Progress in Grammar, Punctuation and Spelling Assessment

MANUAL STAGE 2
Years 3–6

✚ MARK

RS✱ASSESSMENT
FROM HODDER EDUCATION

Although every effort has been made to ensure that website addresses are correct at time of going to press, RS Assessment from Hodder Education cannot be held responsible for the content of any website mentioned in this book. It is sometimes possible to find a relocated web page by typing in the address of the home page for a website in the URL window of your browser.

Orders: please contact Bookpoint Ltd, 130 Park Drive, Milton Park, Abingdon, Oxon OX14 4SE. Telephone: (44) 01235 400555. Email: primary@bookpoint.co.uk.

Lines are open from 9 a.m. to 5 p.m., Monday to Saturday, with a 24-hour message answering service. Visit our website at www.rsassessment.com for details of other assessment publications.

Online support and queries email: onlinesupport@risingstars-uk.com.

ISBN: 978 1 47188 504 4

© Rising Stars UK Ltd 2018

First published in 2018 by
RS Assessment from Hodder Education, part of the Hodder Education Group
An Hachette UK Company
Carmelite House
50 Victoria Embankment
London EC4Y 0DZ

www.rsassessment.com

Impression number   10 9 8 7 6 5 4 3 2

Year   2022 2021 2020 2019 2018

Progress in Grammar, Punctuation and Spelling Assessment developed by Alpha*Plus* Consultancy Ltd.

Author and review team: Annabel Charles, Becky Clarkson, Alissa McDonald, Claire Metcalfe, Kate Ruttle, Romy Short, Siobhan Skeffington.

All rights reserved. Apart from any use permitted under UK copyright law, the material in this publication is copyright and cannot be photocopied or otherwise produced in its entirety or copied onto acetate without permission. Electronic copying is not permitted. Permission is given to teachers to make copies of individual pages marked © Rising Stars UK Ltd 2018. You may photocopy this sheet, for classroom distribution only, to pupils within their own school or educational institution. The material may not be copied in unlimited quantities, kept on behalf of others, distributed outside the purchasing institution, copied onwards, sold to third parties, or stored for future use in a retrieval system. This permission is subject to the payment of the purchase price of the book. If you wish to use the material in any way other than as specified you must apply in writing to the Publisher at the above address.

Typeset in India

Printed in the UK

A catalogue record for this title is available from the British Library.

gaps

Contents

1 Introduction — 5
Why use *GaPS*? — 5
Curriculum maps and progression in *GaPS* — 6
GaPS online analysis and reports — 7
Monitoring and predicting progress using *GaPS* — 7
When to use each *GaPS* test — 8
Performance indicators — 9
Who can you assess using *GaPS*? — 10

2 Administering the *GaPS* tests — 11
When to test — 11
Group size — 11
Timing — 11
Preparation — 11
Administering the test — 11
Spelling test transcripts — 12

3 Answers and mark schemes — 25
Marking the answers — 25
Finding the total raw score — 25
Profiling performance by strand — 25
Obtaining other scores — 25
Answers and mark schemes for each test (including facilities for each question) — 27
Record Sheet for each test (photocopiable) — 106

4 Test scores — 110
Summative measures — 110
Diagnostic and formative interpretation — 117
Reporting progress using the Hodder Scale — 118
Predicting future performance with the Hodder Scale — 118
Case studies — 120

5 Technical information — 123
Standardisation sample — 123
Reliability — 123
Validity — 126

6 Standardised score tables — 127
Standardised scores, Hodder Scale scores and GPS ages for *GaPS* — 127
Age-standardised scores for *GaPS* — 139

Acknowledgements

The authors and publishers would like to thank the staff and pupils from the following schools that took part in trialling in Autumn 2016 and Spring and Summer 2017.

Alderman Cogan's Church of England Primary Academy, Hull

All Saints Primary School Runcorn, Runcorn

Anglesey Primary School, Burton-upon-Trent

Castleton Primary School, Leeds

Cedar Children's Academy, Rochester

Dean Bank Primary and Nursery School, Ferryhill

Denbigh Primary School, Luton

Emmer Green Primary School, Reading

Garswood Primary and Nursery School, Garswood

Madley Primary School, Hereford

The Marist Catholic Primary School, West Byfleet

Marhamchurch CofE VC Primary School, Marhamchurch

Markington CE Primary School, Markington

Melbury Primary School, Nottingham

Moortown Primary School, Leeds

Our Lady of the Rosary RC VA Primary School, Bristol

Penn Wood Primary and Nursery School, Slough

Riverside Community Primary School and Nursery, Plymouth

Saints Peter and Paul Catholic Primary School, Coventry

Scholes (Elmet) Primary School, Leeds

Springfield Primary School, Derby

St. Anselm's Catholic Primary School, Harrow

St. Charles RC Primary School, Blackburn

St. Edmund's Roman Catholic Primary School, Manchester

St. James' Church of England Primary School, Wetherby

St. John's CE (C) Primary School, Keele

St. Joseph's Preparatory School, Stoke-on-Trent

St. Mary Cray Primary Academy, Orpington

St. Paul's CE Primary School, Salford

St. White's Primary School, Cinderford

Trowell CofE Primary School, Nottingham

Vauxhall Primary School, London

The Westborough School, Southend-on-Sea

Woodland View Junior School, Norwich

gaps

1 Introduction

Progress in Grammar, Punctuation and Spelling (GaPS) provides a termly standardised assessment of a pupil's English language and spelling attainment, plus a profile of grammar, punctuation, vocabulary and spelling skills, which helps you identify those pupils who may need further teaching and practice. Separate tests are available for the Autumn, Spring and Summer terms for each of Years 1 to 6. *GaPS* is designed for whole-class use, with pupils of all abilities. The *GaPS* tests are designed to be used just after half-term, but may also be used towards the end of each term in each primary school year in order to measure and monitor pupils' progress and to provide reliable predictive and diagnostic information. The tests are simple and quick to administer, and straightforward to mark. Each test takes between 40 and 50 minutes, depending on the year group, and each test is divided into two parts – one for grammar, punctuation and vocabulary and the other for spelling – which can be administered separately.

GaPS tests assess the 2014 National Curriculum and the content domain-assessable elements of the 2015 English grammar, punctuation and spelling test frameworks published by the Standards and Testing Agency for National Curriculum Tests. The *GaPS* tests provide thorough coverage of the National Curriculum 2014 Programme of Study for each year. This has been assured by systematically sampling Key Stage 1 and Key Stage 2 performance descriptors for English using the 2015 test frameworks and being informed by the Key Stage 1 and Key Stage 2 national tests.

A large-scale standardisation trial (involving over 30 schools and over 6000 pupils) was undertaken for *GaPS* between September 2016 and July 2017, with nationally representative groups of pupils, to produce the data tables provided in this manual. This enables schools to have confidence in the information provided from these new tests. Further details about this process are provided in Chapter 5 *Technical information*.

Why use *GaPS*?

Using *GaPS* provides many benefits. First, *GaPS* gives reliable summative information, for example:

- if you want to follow the progress of your pupils from term to term, as well as year to year through the primary school, *GaPS* provides *three* carefully designed tests for each year;

- if you wish to set appropriate and meaningful targets for your pupils, and to evaluate their progress, *GaPS* tests provide an empirical basis on which to do so;

- if you need to have an external reference for your value-added requirements, *GaPS* tests supply it.

Second, *GaPS* also has a diagnostic capability, enabling you to investigate the strengths and weaknesses of your pupils' language skills across grammar, punctuation, vocabulary and spelling (Table 1.1).

Table 1.1 Strands used in *GaPS*

Strand	Description
G	Grammar
P	Punctuation
V	Vocabulary
S	Spelling

You can also examine the performance of pupils on each question. Using the percentage of pupils who answered each question correctly in the national standardisation (the facility value), you can easily compare the performance of your own pupils with those in the national sample. You will find facility values by each question in the relevant mark scheme.

GaPS will help you answer parents, governors, inspectors or headteachers who ask questions such as:

- How has *my* child done compared to others of his/her age or year group?
- What pattern of performance do pupils in a particular year typically achieve?
- Has this pupil made good progress from year to year?
- What would be a reasonable level of achievement for this pupil next term?
- What are the strengths of this pupil, or class?
- What individual and class *targets* are appropriate and realistic?
- On what aspects of language should this pupil focus to maximise progress?
- What would constitute good, average or poor progress for this pupil, or class?
- What is my child's GPS age?

This manual contains all the information you need to obtain standardised scores, age-standardised scores, percentiles, grammar, punctuation, vocabulary and spelling age, a score on the Hodder Scale together with age-related performance indicators for the end of year and a profile of performance against strands. All together, the various scores provide a wealth of information that will support you in managing learning in your classroom.

Curriculum maps and progression in *GaPS*

The *GaPS* tests provide thorough coverage of the National Curriculum 2014 Programme of Study for the particular year.

The *GaPS* curriculum maps (available for free at www.risingstars-uk.com/gaps-curriculum-maps) take in the 2014 Programme of Study, which describes what should be covered by the end of each year, and how the teaching of the material might be allocated to each term. For a test to give reliable results, it needs to be valid – that is, to assess what has been taught – so the curriculum maps define what *GaPS* assesses each term.

The *GaPS* curriculum map for each term will help in planning your teaching. The curriculum maps have been designed to break down the national curriculum into a meaningful term-by-term programme of study, breaking down skills and content into termly 'chunks'. These maps have been designed so that skills and content get progressively more difficult over the terms and years of Key Stage 2. Similarly the tests have been designed to assess this progressively more difficult content and to build upon assessments from the previous terms and years. The maps are designed to cover all necessary content in a meaningful progression so that pupils are at the expected point in their learning when they reach the end of Key Stage 2 national tests.

GaPS online analysis and reports

If you are using the pencil-and-paper tests, the online analysis and reporting tool on MARK (My Assessment and Reporting Kit) will enable you to analyse group performance (for example, by class and/or gender), track pupil performance through the school and generate individual progress predictions. See page 26 for more information.

Monitoring and predicting progress using *GaPS*

GaPS tests give you five distinct types of information to inform you of the progress of each child, class and cohort:

- **standardised scores**, which show how a learner's score relates to national performance;
- **age-standardised scores**, which take into account a child's chronological age so that you can see how a child's performance compares with other children of the same age;
- **grammar, punctuation, vocabulary and spelling age** for a quick at-a-glance reference;
- **performance indicators**, giving relative attainment term on term;
- the **Hodder Scale**, which is an independent measure of progress throughout primary.

The use of each of these scores is explained more fully in Chapter 4 *Test scores*.

The *GaPS* test results have been statistically linked from term to term and year to year, to allow progress to be measured across the different terms and years. Results from the test enable you to monitor strengths and weaknesses and track progress through the whole primary phase. The information provided in this manual enables you to monitor and compare in detail individual patterns of performance against the norms and patterns for the term or year.

The Hodder Scale acts as a common 'spine' on which are plotted all of the *GaPS* tests across the whole primary phase (Table 4.5 on pages 119–20 shows this scale across Key Stage 2). It provides the statistical basis for *predicting* pupil progress and future attainment, based on the termly performance data of over 6000 pupils nationally.

The Hodder Scale, as a fixed reference point, has the virtue of being a secure standard with a proven history. It is directly related to the raw scores in *GaPS* and does not take age into account. Teachers can use the results from a *GaPS* test, the Hodder Scale, age-standardised scores and standardised score information together with the performance indicator band to provide clear evidence of how well pupils are doing with their grammar, punctuation and spelling from term to term.

Many teachers wish to be able to use the results from *GaPS* tests to find out if their pupils are working at the expected standard for the term. This information can be calculated from the standardised score, using the bands in Table 1.2 on page 9.

Profiling test scores

The photocopiable *GaPS* Record Sheets on pages 106–9 will enable you to profile scores and analyse pupils' performance in the different grammar, punctuation and spelling strands. You can then evaluate their progress relative to national average performance (shown by the tints) for each aspect of grammar, punctuation and spelling to see if there are patterns of strengths and weaknesses. (See 'Profiling performance by strand' on page 25 for further details.)

You may also go one stage further and check a pupil's individual performance on a specific question and compare how they have performed relative to other pupils in the same year group. Refer to the mark scheme to see what proportion of pupils in that year group answered each question correctly. This is called the *facility* and is shown as a percentage: 60 per cent shows that 60 per cent of pupils in the national sample answered the question correctly.

If you wish, you can also average your pupils' scores to create an overall *class* or *cohort* profile. The pattern revealed may inform both teaching and target setting, as it will highlight the grammar, punctuation and spelling skills in which pupils are secure or confident and those that need further support and practice. Alternatively, input the scores into MARK for automatic profile reporting (see page 26).

When to use each *GaPS* test

GaPS provides the most useful information if it is used termly. However, if necessary, it can be used just once every year. The tests for years 3 and 4 each contain 45 marks and the tests for years 5 and 6 each contain 55 marks with all the tests assessing different elements from the national curriculum. Section A of each test includes a range of questions assessing grammar, punctuation and vocabulary relevant to each term as set out in the *GaPS* curriculum map. Section B of each test assesses spelling rules and words from the word list set out in the curriculum map. The tests should be taken when the relevant content has been taught; this may vary depending on the school's own schemes of work.

The Key Stage 2 *GaPS* tests are able to provide a profile of the performance of your pupils in the core skills and content that underpin progress in grammar, punctuation, vocabulary and spelling, enabling you to focus your attention on supporting them as they develop the most important skills.

Performance indicators

The performance indicators reflect where pupils, groups, classes and the schools are in relation to other schools term on term. We have developed the following performance indicators to provide you with information about relative performance each term.

Table 1.2: Performance indicator bands

Performance indicator	Standardised score
Working towards	<94
Working at	94–114
Working at greater depth	>114

This measure is based on the standards calculated from the performance of ournational representative standardisation sample. The standardisation has set the average score at 100, with 15 marks each side of this being one standard deviation. That is 68% of pupils would fall between a standardised score of 85 and 115. The levels set here are set such that schools are expected to generally be better than the national average. This is to ensure that they are on track to achieve the required standards at Key Stage 2. The 'working at greater depth' standard is set so that 16% of learners will achieve this.

Children with standardised scores just below or just above 94–95 may be considered on the cusp of the performance indicator band. The performance of children on the cusp is always less predictable than those who achieve scores comfortably within the expected standard. We want to ensure that we don't overinflate the performance of children on the cusp, so we have set the performance indicator band for 'Working at' to be slightly more demanding than the national test expected standard.

These performance indicator bands may be used for tests in each term to measure if a child is on track to achieve an expected standard at the end of the year and to aggregate performance for groups, classes and years. These performance indicators will be available as part of the online analysis and reporting service (see page 25 for more information).

If a child achieves the 'working at greater depth' performance indicator band in a test, they won't necessarily be predicted 'working at greater depth' in the next test. This is because the Hodder scale score table is based on actual pupil performance and this pattern shows that children with similar performances sometimes fall below the 'working at greater depth' band on the next test. This seems to be prevalent for Autumn to Spring predictions. In Autumn there is recap of the previous year's curriculum, whereas the Spring test will have more questions of the current year's curriculum. There may also be more questions at greater depth within the Spring curriculum, meaning that the Spring test provides a greater challenge. In any given test only a few marks will fall within the 'working at greater depth' performance indicator band, so the judgement of 'working at greater depth' has to be seen as indicative rather than totally secure. For a secure judgement of 'working at greater depth' there needs to be a greater array of evidence.

Who can you assess using *GaPS*?

The spread of demand of the tests allows you to use each test with wide-ability groups, including weaker pupils, and allows all pupils to experience some success.

Very low attaining pupils may benefit from taking tests intended for earlier terms or years, where they are more likely to experience success and be able to demonstrate what they know and understand, rather than struggle with questions that are too demanding for them. In a similar way, high attaining pupils following an extension or accelerated pathway may take tests intended for older age groups, which will provide evidence of them working at greater depth as they will meet more difficult questions.

Please note that it may not be possible to obtain an age-standardised score or percentile when the tests are used in this way, if the pupil is outside the chronological age range of the conversion table for the test used. However, you may be able to get a GPS age, and will be able to get a Hodder Scale score.

2 Administering the *GaPS* tests

When to test

The *GaPS* tests should ideally be used shortly after the relevant half-term, since this exactly mirrors the time they were taken in the trialling and will therefore give the most dependable data. However, in practice, using the tests one or two months either side of this optimum point is unlikely to be critical. This pattern also provides objective information for the pupil progress meetings and data-collection points which most schools have at around half-term.

Using the *GaPS* tests earlier rather than later in the second half of term can help the results to feed into and inform classroom practice or be used for end-of-term reporting.

Group size

You can administer the tests to whole classes or large groups if you feel comfortable doing so, but with weaker Year 3 children it may be better with small groups. Some teachers find it more effective to work with small groups – say five or six children of similar ability – so that a break can be taken if required.

Timing

A maximum time limit of 40–50 minutes is set for the Key Stage 2 *GaPS* tests. For Years 3 and 4 the grammar, punctuation and vocabulary section of the test is likely to take 25 minutes. For Years 5 and 6, 30 minutes. The spelling tests for all year groups will take between 15 and 20 minutes. You may want to allow a break between the two sections of the test.

Preparation

Each pupil will need a copy of the appropriate test booklet plus a pencil or pen and an eraser. Answers may be altered by crossing or rubbing out.

Administering the test

Ask pupils to write their name, gender, date of birth and test date on the front of the test booklet. If any pupils are not clear about what they have to do, you may give additional explanation to help them understand the requirements of the test. If a child needs further help you may read the Section A questions aloud but do not help with individual words, if they are unable to understand they should move on to the next question.

If the results are to be reliable, it is important that the pupils work alone, without copying from each other or discussing their answers.

Before pupils complete Section A of the test (grammar, punctuation and vocabulary), explain the following key points to them:

- the answer booklet consists of a range of questions: children should attempt them all;

- if children find a question too hard, they should have a go and then move on to the next one: they should not spend too long on questions they cannot answer;
- if children have problems, they should ask for help by raising their hand;
- children have approximately 25–30 minutes to complete the first part of the test depending on which year they are in;
- if they finish before then, they should go back and check their work.

After pupils have completed Section A of the test move on to Section B (spelling). You may wish to administer this after the children have had a break. Ensure that all children are on the correct page in their test booklet and explain the following key points:

- that for the spelling section of the test you are going to read out 20 sentences to them;
- each sentence has a word missing on their answer sheet;
- they should listen carefully to the missing word and write the word, making sure they spell it correctly, on the line within the sentence in their test booklets;
- you will read the word, then the word within a sentence and then repeat the word a third time.

Spelling test transcripts

Pages 13–24 contain the transcripts for the spelling tests which you should read aloud. There are 20 words in the test. You should introduce each word with the sentence 'The word is "xxx"'. Then read the sentence with the word included in the sentence and then finally repeat the sentence 'The word is "xxx"'.

GaPS 3 Autumn: Spelling test transcript

Qn	Teacher script
1	Spelling 1: The word is **busy**. The squirrels were **busy** burying their food. The word is **busy**.
2	Spelling 2: The word is **wrist**. Your **wrist** joins your hand to your arm. The word is **wrist**.
3	Spelling 3: The word is **parents**. The **parents** came to watch the school play. The word is **parents**.
4	Spelling 4: The word is **grass**. In spring, the **grass** is green. The word is **grass**.
5	Spelling 5: The word is **group**. I am in red **group** for reading. The word is **group**.
6	Spelling 6: The word is **sentence**. Think of a **sentence** to describe a cat. The word is **sentence**.
7	Spelling 7: The word is **young**. Hari is too **young** to play with us. The word is **young**.
8	Spelling 8: The word is **fruit**. We eat **fruit** at snack time. The word is **fruit**.
9	Spelling 9: The word is **heart**. Your **heart** pumps your blood round your body. The word is **heart**.
10	Spelling 10: The word is **learn**. Did you **learn** your three times table? The word is **learn**.

Qn	Teacher script
11	Spelling 11: The word is **double**. Ten is the same as **double** five. The word is **double**.
12	Spelling 12: The word is **quarter**. My sister gave me a **quarter** of her cake. The word is **quarter**.
13	Spelling 13: The word is **veins**. The **veins** in my arm look blue. The word is **veins**.
14	Spelling 14: The word is **consider**. Did you **consider** all the choices in the question? The word is **consider**.
15	Spelling 15: The word is **straight**. A square has four **straight** sides. The word is **straight**.
16	Spelling 16: The word is **characters**. Some stories have too many **characters**. The word is **characters**.
17	Spelling 17: The word is **weight**. The little cat's **weight** was a surprise. The word is **weight**.
18	Spelling 18: The word is **caught**. I **caught** the ball and threw it back. The word is **caught**.
19	Spelling 19: The word is **disappear**. I can make this apple **disappear**. The word is **disappear**.
20	Spelling 20: The word is **myth**. A **myth** is a kind of story. The word is **myth**.

GaPS 3 Spring: Spelling test transcript

Qn	Teacher script
1	Spelling 1: The word is **biggest**. The **biggest** is not always the best. The word is **biggest**.
2	Spelling 2: The word is **grate**. The fire was burning in the **grate**. The word is **grate**.
3	Spelling 3: The word is **decide**. What did you **decide**? The word is **decide**.
4	Spelling 4: The word is **thought**. Tell me what you **thought**. The word is **thought**.
5	Spelling 5: The word is **hear**. Can you **hear** me? The word is **hear**.
6	Spelling 6: The word is **gently**. Ayla **gently** stroked the kitten. The word is **gently**.
7	Spelling 7: The word is **happiest**. The **happiest** person won a prize. The word is **happiest**.
8	Spelling 8: The word is **remember**. Can you **remember** your phone number? The word is **remember**.
9	Spelling 9: The word is **heaviest**. My grandad grew the **heaviest** pumpkin. The word is **heaviest**.
10	Spelling 10: The word is **possible**. It is always **possible** to learn. The word is **possible**.

Qn	Teacher script
11	Spelling 11: The word is **through**. The train went **through** the tunnel. The word is **through**.
12	Spelling 12: The word is **centre**. Do you live near a sports **centre**? The word is **centre**.
13	Spelling 13: The word is **decorations**. We are making **decorations** for the school. The word is **decorations**.
14	Spelling 14: The word is **forwards**. Hit the ball **forwards** to your partner. The word is **forwards**.
15	Spelling 15: The word is **height**. Your **height** means how tall you are. The word is **height**.
16	Spelling 16: The word is **information**. Listen carefully to the **information**. The word is **information**.
17	Spelling 17: The word is **popular**. People who are **popular** have lots of friends. The word is **popular**.
18	Spelling 18: The word is **tomatoes**. It is easy to grow **tomatoes**. The word is **tomatoes**.
19	Spelling 19: The word is **particular**. You need to take **particular** care today. The word is **particular**.
20	Spelling 20: The word is **although**. I will eat rice **although** I prefer pasta. The word is **although**.

GaPS 3 Summer: Spelling test transcript

Qn	Teacher script
1	Spelling 1: The word is **Thursday**. **Thursday** is my favourite day. The word is **Thursday**.
2	Spelling 2: The word is **address**. My **address** tells people where I live. The word is **address**.
3	Spelling 3: The word is **usually**. We **usually** go swimming on Mondays. The word is **usually**.
4	Spelling 4: The word is **describe**. How would you **describe** yourself? The word is **describe**.
5	Spelling 5: The word is **although**. I like peanut butter **although** I don't like peanuts. The word is **although**.
6	Spelling 6: The word is **appear**. You **appear** to be very happy at school. The word is **appear**.
7	Spelling 7: The word is **particular**. Which **particular** puppy do you like best? The word is **particular**.
8	Spelling 8: The word is **investigation**. We did an **investigation** in science. The word is **investigation**.
9	Spelling 9: The word is **complete**. We will have a break once we **complete** this assessment. The word is **complete**.
10	Spelling 10: The word is **misheard**. Lola **misheard** what the teacher said. The word is **misheard**.

Qn	Teacher script
11	Spelling 11: The word is **rewrite**. Simon had to **rewrite** his messy work. The word is **rewrite**.
12	Spelling 12: The word is **February**. The month after January is **February**. The word is **February**.
13	Spelling 13: The word is **perhaps**. **Perhaps** we should take our umbrellas with us today. The word is **perhaps**.
14	Spelling 14: The word is **arrive**. Will you let me know when they **arrive**? The word is **arrive**.
15	Spelling 15: The word is **actually**. He is **actually** getting a quad bike. The word is **actually**.
16	Spelling 16: The word is **impossible**. Do you think that will be **impossible**? The word is **impossible**.
17	Spelling 17: The word is **scene**. Artur liked the **scene** when the pirates came on stage. The word is **scene**.
18	Spelling 18: The word is **relaxation**. For **relaxation**, he loved to read. The word is **relaxation**.
19	Spelling 19: The word is **disagreement**. Luke had a **disagreement** with his best friend. The word is **disagreement**.
20	Spelling 20: The word is **improve**. If I work hard at anything, I will **improve**. The word is **improve**.

GaPS 4 Autumn: Spelling test transcript

Qn	Teacher script
1	Spelling 1: The word is **slowly**. Shania hopped **slowly** on one leg. The word is **slowly**.
2	Spelling 2: The word is **August**. The school is closed in **August**. The word is **August**.
3	Spelling 3: The word is **smaller**. The glove was **smaller** than his hand. The word is **smaller**.
4	Spelling 4: The word is **important**. It is **important** to brush your teeth. The word is **important**.
5	Spelling 5: The word is **automobile**. An old-fashioned word for a car is **automobile**. The word is **automobile**.
6	Spelling 6: The word is **inactive**. The volcano had been **inactive** for hundreds of years. The word is **inactive**.
7	Spelling 7: The word is **impolite**. Joshua was **impolite** to his teacher. The word is **impolite**.
8	Spelling 8: The word is **machine**. I would like to invent a brand new **machine**. The word is **machine**.
9	Spelling 9: The word is **unique**. Efe's colourful outfit for the carnival was **unique**. The word is **unique**.
10	Spelling 10: The word is **build**. You can **build** a tower of bricks. The word is **build**.

Qn	Teacher script
11	Spelling 11: The word is **believe**. That story is hard to **believe**. The word is **believe**.
12	Spelling 12: The word is **imagine**. On a cold day, I love to **imagine** it is summer. The word is **imagine**.
13	Spelling 13: The word is **November**. My favourite month is **November**. The word is **November**.
14	Spelling 14: The word is **breath**. It was so cold I could see my **breath**. The word is **breath**.
15	Spelling 15: The word is **chef**. The **chef** cooked a wonderful meal. The word is **chef**.
16	Spelling 16: The word is **circle**. All the children stood in a **circle**. The word is **circle**.
17	Spelling 17: The word is **increase**. You see an **increase** in the number of butterflies in the summer. The word is **increase**.
18	Spelling 18: The word is **strange**. Edward found it **strange** that Mr Green always wore a hat. The word is **strange**.
19	Spelling 19: The word is **scissors**. The teacher said to cut carefully with your **scissors**. The word is **scissors**.
20	Spelling 20: The word is **guide**. Some people can use the stars as a **guide** to find their way. The word is **guide**.

GaPS 4 Spring: Spelling test transcript

Qn	Teacher script
1	Spelling 1: The word is **often**. Sabrina **often** visits the library. The word is **often**.
2	Spelling 2: The word is **subheading**. The story in the newspaper had a funny **subheading**. The word is **subheading**.
3	Spelling 3: The word is **superstar**. The crowd was waiting to see the **superstar**. The word is **superstar**.
4	Spelling 4: The word is **destination**. The train's **destination** is Manchester. The word is **destination**.
5	Spelling 5: The word is **pleasure**. It would be my **pleasure** to help you. The word is **pleasure**.
6	Spelling 6: The word is **misbehave**. "We never **misbehave**," said the twins. The word is **misbehave**.
7	Spelling 7: The word is **nature**. My sister loves animals and everything to do with **nature**. The word is **nature**.
8	Spelling 8: The word is **picture**. Zak made a **picture** out of pasta. The word is **picture**.
9	Spelling 9: The word is **therefore**. I love to grow plants, and **therefore** I will buy some seeds. The word is **therefore**.
10	Spelling 10: The word is **island**. In Japan, there is an **island** where only rabbits live. The word is **island**.

Qn	Teacher script
11	Spelling 11: The word is **vision**. People say eating carrots helps your **vision**. The word is **vision**.
12	Spelling 12: The word is **promise**. It can be hard to keep a **promise**. The word is **promise**.
13	Spelling 13: The word is **confusion**. The wrong ticket caused **confusion**. The word is **confusion**.
14	Spelling 14: The word is **peace**. Early in the morning, I love the **peace** and quiet. The word is **peace**.
15	Spelling 15: The word is **treasure**. Hanni and Stefan pretended their stones were **treasure**. The word is **treasure**.
16	Spelling 16: The word is **mission**. The astronauts were sent on a **mission** to the moon. The word is **mission**.
17	Spelling 17: The word is **experiment**. Class 4B did an **experiment** about forces. The word is **experiment**.
18	Spelling 18: The word is **material**. Silk is a delicate **material**. The word is **material**.
19	Spelling 19: The word is **enclosure**. The animals were moved to a larger **enclosure**. The word is **enclosure**.
20	Spelling 20: The word is **musician**. My father is a teacher and my mother is a **musician**. The word is **musician**.

GaPS 4 Summer: Spelling test transcript

Qn	Teacher script
1	Spelling 1: The word is **medal**. Every child in the swimming team won a **medal**. The word is **medal**.
2	Spelling 2: The word is **revision**. A **revision** was made to the school timetable. The word is **revision**.
3	Spelling 3: The word is **creature**. The explorer discovered a new **creature**. The word is **creature**.
4	Spelling 4: The word is **hesitation**. The player hit the ball without **hesitation**. The word is **hesitation**.
5	Spelling 5: The word is **interest**. Paula lost **interest** in the game. The word is **interest**.
6	Spelling 6: The word is **dangerous**. Don't go too close to the edge, it's **dangerous**. The word is **dangerous**.
7	Spelling 7: The word is **length**. We measured the **length** of the playground. The word is **length**.
8	Spelling 8: The word is **finally**. Chris was very happy as the holidays were **finally** here. The word is **finally**.
9	Spelling 9: The word is **enormous**. An **enormous** crowd had gathered to see the performer. The word is **enormous**.
10	Spelling 10: The word is **forgetting**. Morgan kept **forgetting** to post his friend's birthday card. The word is **forgetting**.

Qn	Teacher script
11	Spelling 11: The word is **opposite**. The pet shop was on the **opposite** side of the road. The word is **opposite**.
12	Spelling 12: The word is **poisonous**. Toadstools are often **poisonous**. The word is **poisonous**.
13	Spelling 13: The word is **strength**. The engineer tested the **strength** of the bridge. The word is **strength**.
14	Spelling 14: The word is **interact**. "These two chemicals **interact** and change colour," said the teacher. The word is **interact**.
15	Spelling 15: The word is **occasion**. The school play was a special **occasion**. The word is **occasion**.
16	Spelling 16: The word is **ordinary**. The cover made the book look very **ordinary**. The word is **ordinary**.
17	Spelling 17: The word is **purpose**. Alma was sure her brother hid her book on **purpose**. The word is **purpose**.
18	Spelling 18: The word is **different**. The shops were very **different** from how she remembered them. The word is **different**.
19	Spelling 19: The word is **favourite**. Snap was still one of Sam's **favourite** games. The word is **favourite**.
20	Spelling 20: The word is **incorrect**. The weather forecast was **incorrect**. The word is **incorrect**.

GaPS 5 Autumn: Spelling test transcript

Qn	Teacher script
1	Spelling 1: The word is **oversleep**. If we **oversleep** we will miss our flight. The word is **oversleep**.
2	Spelling 2: The word is **rough**. The ship had problems on the **rough** sea. The word is **rough**.
3	Spelling 3: The word is **excellent**. Raj did some **excellent** work on the Tudors. The word is **excellent**.
4	Spelling 4: The word is **importance**. The theatre visit was an event of great **importance**. The word is **importance**.
5	Spelling 5: The word is **innocence**. The man had to prove his **innocence**. The word is **innocence**.
6	Spelling 6: The word is **classify**. Our task was to **classify** insects. The word is **classify**.
7	Spelling 7: The word is **mislead**. The politician did not mean to **mislead** the audience. The word is **mislead**.
8	Spelling 8: The word is **restructure**. Our plan was to **restructure** the class assembly. The word is **restructure**.
9	Spelling 9: The word is **disappeared**. The snowman **disappeared** after the first sunny day. The word is **disappeared**.
10	Spelling 10: The word is **deactivate**. I had to **deactivate** the alien's laser gun. The word is **deactivate**.

Qn	Teacher script
11	Spelling 11: The word is **musician**. The **musician** was excellent. The word is **musician**.
12	Spelling 12: The word is **invention**. The **invention** was a big success. The word is **invention**.
13	Spelling 13: The word is **division**. We learnt about long **division** in maths. The word is **division**.
14	Spelling 14: The word is **measure**. I had to **measure** five objects in class. The word is **measure**.
15	Spelling 15: The word is **humorous**. The poem used a lot of **humorous** language. The word is **humorous**.
16	Spelling 16: The word is **justify**. You need to **justify** your reasons. The word is **justify**.
17	Spelling 17: The word is **revisit**. I would like to **revisit** Glasgow one day. The word is **revisit**.
18	Spelling 18: The word is **characterise**. We had to **characterise** King Henry VIII. The word is **characterise**.
19	Spelling 19: The word is **disallow**. The referee decided to **disallow** the goal. The word is **disallow**.
20	Spelling 20: The word is **development**. The shopping centre **development** was going slowly. The word is **development**.

2 Administering the *GaPS* tests

GaPS 5 Spring: Spelling test transcript

Qn	Teacher script
1	Spelling 1: The word is **disarm**. I was able to **disarm** the alarm by typing in the right code. The word is **disarm**.
2	Spelling 2: The word is **declutter**. My mum told me to **declutter** my room. The word is **declutter**.
3	Spelling 3: The word is **entrance**. The school **entrance** was closed. The word is **entrance**.
4	Spelling 4: The word is **tough**. The homework we were given was **tough** to complete. The word is **tough**.
5	Spelling 5: The word is **confident**. I was **confident** I would win the prize. The word is **confident**.
6	Spelling 6: The word is **disconnect**. We had to **disconnect** the electricity. The word is **disconnect**.
7	Spelling 7: The word is **reliably**. Amy was always **reliably** on time for art club. The word is **reliably**.
8	Spelling 8: The word is **available**. The new scooter model was **available** at the local shop. The word is **available**.
9	Spelling 9: The word is **sensibly**. Ali was dressed **sensibly** for the weather. The word is **sensibly**.
10	Spelling 10: The word is **knight**. The **knight** was very brave. The word is **knight**.

Qn	Teacher script
11	Spelling 11: The word is **temperature**. My little sister had a high **temperature**. The word is **temperature**.
12	Spelling 12: The word is **stomach**. I had a **stomach** ache all afternoon. The word is **stomach**.
13	Spelling 13: The word is **according**. I was late **according** to the classroom clock. The word is **according**.
14	Spelling 14: The word is **desperate**. I was **desperate** to win the race. The word is **desperate**.
15	Spelling 15: The word is **observant**. She watched the play with an **observant** eye. The word is **observant**.
16	Spelling 16: The word is **whistle**. My dad can **whistle** very well. The word is **whistle**.
17	Spelling 17: The word is **misinform**. I did not mean to **misinform** my friend. The word is **misinform**.
18	Spelling 18: The word is **dependable**. Josh is a **dependable** classmate. The word is **dependable**.
19	Spelling 19: The word is **specialises**. The publisher **specialises** in children's books. The word is **specialises**.
20	Spelling 20: The word is **appearance**. The young man had a scruffy **appearance**. The word is **appearance**.

GaPS 5 Summer: Spelling test transcript

Qn	Teacher script
1	Spelling 1: The word is **develop**. I need to **develop** my throwing technique. The word is **develop**.
2	Spelling 2: The word is **rebuild**. We had to **rebuild** our model bridge. The word is **rebuild**.
3	Spelling 3: The word is **deceived**. She was **deceived** by the book's cover. The word is **deceived**.
4	Spelling 4: The word is **community**. Our local **community** group planted lots of trees. The word is **community**.
5	Spelling 5: The word is **supervise**. The year 6 children were able to **supervise** at playtime. The word is **supervise**.
6	Spelling 6: The word is **antibiotics**. Rob was given **antibiotics** by the doctor. The word is **antibiotics**.
7	Spelling 7: The word is **doubt**. I **doubt** he will finish his work. The word is **doubt**.
8	Spelling 8: The word is **simplify**. The teacher had to **simplify** his explanation. The word is **simplify**.
9	Spelling 9: The word is **misidentified**. The gardener **misidentified** the flowers. The word is **misidentified**.
10	Spelling 10: The word is **discontinue**. The students were told to **discontinue** the newspaper. The word is **discontinue**.

Qn	Teacher script
11	Spelling 11: The word is **definite**. We had no **definite** plans for the weekend. The word is **definite**.
12	Spelling 12: The word is **immediate**. My enjoyment of the music was **immediate**. The word is **immediate**.
13	Spelling 13: The word is **weary**. I was **weary** after doing PE all afternoon. The word is **weary**.
14	Spelling 14: The word is **signature**. The painter's **signature** was clear to see. The word is **signature**.
15	Spelling 15: The word is **symbols**. My sister uses lots of **symbols** in her texts. The word is **symbols**.
16	Spelling 16: The word is **bruise**. I had a big **bruise** on my knee. The word is **bruise**.
17	Spelling 17: The word is **attached**. My keys are **attached** to a key ring. The word is **attached**.
18	Spelling 18: The word is **perceived**. Mrs Smith quickly **perceived** the truth. The word is **perceived**.
19	Spelling 19: The word is **curious**. I was **curious** to see what was in the box. The word is **curious**.
20	Spelling 20: The word is **twelfth**. I was **twelfth** in the queue. The word is **twelfth**.

2 Administering the *GaPS* tests

GaPS 6 Autumn: Spelling test transcript

Qn	Teacher script
1	Spelling 1: The word is **automatic**. John went through the **automatic** door of the shop. The word is **automatic**.
2	Spelling 2: The word is **bargain**. The cheap shoes were a **bargain**. The word is **bargain**.
3	Spelling 3: The word is **programme**. Eva watched her favourite television **programme**. The word is **programme**.
4	Spelling 4: The word is **disappear**. The children saw the kitten **disappear** behind the tree. The word is **disappear**.
5	Spelling 5: The word is **ambitious**. Mrs Khan is very **ambitious** for her son. The word is **ambitious**.
6	Spelling 6: The word is **suspicious**. The old lady was behaving in a **suspicious** way. The word is **suspicious**.
7	Spelling 7: The word is **artificial**. The orange juice tasted **artificial**. The word is **artificial**.
8	Spelling 8: The word is **leisure**. Are you going to the **leisure** centre today? The word is **leisure**.
9	Spelling 9: The word is **queue**. Everyone had to **queue** to get onto the bus. The word is **queue**.
10	Spelling 10: The word is **exaggerate**. Mr Jones told us not to **exaggerate**. The word is **exaggerate**.

Qn	Teacher script
11	Spelling 11: The word is **opportunity**. I had the **opportunity** to play for England. The word is **opportunity**.
12	Spelling 12: The word is **achievement**. Finishing the model was an **achievement** for Ali. The word is **achievement**.
13	Spelling 13: The word is **determined**. Dina was **determined** to get into the team. The word is **determined**.
14	Spelling 14: The word is **Parliament**. Who would like to visit the Houses of **Parliament**? The word is **Parliament**.
15	Spelling 15: The word is **affect**. Feeling tired can **affect** your ability to work. The word is **affect**.
16	Spelling 16: The word is **environmental**. Read these **environmental** tips for children. The word is **environmental**.
17	Spelling 17: The word is **physically**. Cross-country running is **physically** tough. The word is **physically**.
18	Spelling 18: The word is **criticise**. Try not to **criticise** other children. The word is **criticise**.
19	Spelling 19: The word is **essential**. Sun-cream is **essential** on a hot day. The word is **essential**.
20	Spelling 20: The word is **especially**. I **especially** like chocolate cake. The word is **especially**.

2 Administering the *GaPS* tests

GaPS 6 Spring: Spelling test transcript

Qn	Teacher script
1	Spelling 1: The word is **misunderstood**. Meera **misunderstood** what the teacher said. The word is **misunderstood**.
2	Spelling 2: The word is **luckiest**. She was the **luckiest** girl in the world. The word is **luckiest**.
3	Spelling 3: The word is **application**. Complete the **application** form to join the team. The word is **application**.
4	Spelling 4: The word is **vehicle**. The **vehicle** was parked outside. The word is **vehicle**.
5	Spelling 5: The word is **ancient**. Class 6 visited an **ancient** castle. The word is **ancient**.
6	Spelling 6: The word is **sincerely**. End your letter to Mr Brown with 'Yours **sincerely**'. The word is **sincerely**.
7	Spelling 7: The word is **competition**. Next term there will be an art **competition**. The word is **competition**.
8	Spelling 8: The word is **embarrass**. I don't want to **embarrass** my friend. The word is **embarrass**.
9	Spelling 9: The word is **rhyme**. I like poems that **rhyme**. The word is **rhyme**.
10	Spelling 10: The word is **mischief**. Sam was always getting into **mischief**. The word is **mischief**.

Qn	Teacher script
11	Spelling 11: The word is **persuade**. **Persuade** your friends to help you. The word is **persuade**.
12	Spelling 12: The word is **communication**. Sign language is a kind of **communication**. The word is **communication**.
13	Spelling 13: The word is **disastrous**. It was a **disastrous** school trip. The word is **disastrous**.
14	Spelling 14: The word is **ceiling**. A spider hung from the **ceiling**. The word is **ceiling**.
15	Spelling 15: The word is **system**. The school sound **system** was broken. The word is **system**.
16	Spelling 16: The word is **knight**. The story was about a brave **knight** and a dragon. The word is **knight**.
17	Spelling 17: The word is **occupy**. **Occupy** yourself by helping Mr Green. The word is **occupy**.
18	Spelling 18: The word is **observe**. The children went to the zoo to **observe** the animals. The word is **observe**.
19	Spelling 19: The word is **explanation**. Write your **explanation** in your exercise book. The word is **explanation**.
20	Spelling 20: The word is **hesitation**. She answered the question quickly, without **hesitation**. The word is **hesitation**.

GaPS 6 Summer: Spelling test transcript

Qn	Teacher script	Qn	Teacher script
1	Spelling 1: The word is **father**. My friend's **father** is a firefighter. The word is **father**.	11	Spelling 11: The word is **appreciate**. I **appreciate** the help my teacher gives me. The word is **appreciate**.
2	Spelling 2: The word is **equipment**. Have you got all your **equipment** for school? The word is **equipment**.	12	Spelling 12: The word is **neighbour**. Mum went next door to see our **neighbour**. The word is **neighbour**.
3	Spelling 3: The word is **shoulders**. My dad carries my little sister on his **shoulders**. The word is **shoulders**.	13	Spelling 13: The word is **achieve**. Did you **achieve** your target in maths? The word is **achieve**.
4	Spelling 4: The word is **recognise**. Do you **recognise** the girl who helped you? The word is **recognise**.	14	Spelling 14: The word is **yacht**. My brother has a toy sailing **yacht**. The word is **yacht**.
5	Spelling 5: The word is **rely**. We **rely** on your support for the team. The word is **rely**.	15	Spelling 15: The word is **systematically**. Jo sorted the pencils **systematically**. The word is **systematically**.
6	Spelling 6: The word is **innocent**. She was found **innocent** of eating the last cake. The word is **innocent**.	16	Spelling 16: The word is **controversy**. There was **controversy** over the building of the new school. The word is **controversy**.
7	Spelling 7: The word is **awkward**. It's **awkward** walking with crutches. The word is **awkward**.	17	Spelling 17: The word is **sufficient**. Is there **sufficient** room in the hall for all the children? The word is **sufficient**.
8	Spelling 8: The word is **average**. Layla is taller than **average**. The word is **average**.	18	Spelling 18: The word is **guarantee**. Irena's new watch has a **guarantee**. The word is **guarantee**.
9	Spelling 9: The word is **considerate**. My auntie is a kind, **considerate** person. The word is **considerate**.	19	Spelling 19: The word is **nutritious**. School lunches are very **nutritious**. The word is **nutritious**.
10	Spelling 10: The word is **muscle**. Ben has hurt a **muscle** in his leg. The word is **muscle**.	20	Spelling 20: The word is **necessary**. Warm coats are **necessary** in winter. The word is **necessary**.

gaps 3 Answers and mark schemes

Once the pupil has completed a *GaPS* test, their answers may be marked using the answers and mark schemes found in this chapter.

Marking the answers

- Use the score box in the right-hand margin alongside each question in the test booklets to record marks.
- Please use your professional judgement when marking.
- Any clear indication of the answer is acceptable irrespective of what was asked for, e.g. a tick or a circle. If more answers than required have been circled or ticked, the mark should not be awarded except if it is clearly indicated that an incorrect response was initially made and then corrected.

Finding the total raw score

You can record total marks for the page at the bottom of each page in the test booklets. Then add together the page scores to find each pupil's total raw score and record this in the total marks box on the front cover.

Profiling performance by strand

A code beneath each mark box in Section A indicates which strand the question is assessing: grammar (G), punctuation (P) or vocabulary (V). The questions in Section B all assess spelling so have not been coded. The *GaPS* curriculum maps (see page 6) provide details of how the content allocation of the strands per year and term. The mark schemes also include the STA national test framework code(s) (available from www.gov.uk/government/collections/national-curriculum-assessments-test-frameworks) for each question so that you can see test performance at a more granular level. For *GaPS* code G6.5 has been added and used for Section A questions assessing homophones and near homophones (Years 1-4) and homophones and other words that are often confused (Years 5 and 6).

If you wish to profile the pupil's performance, add up the number of correct answers the pupil has obtained in each strand and record these in the mark boxes on the front cover.

You can make a visual record of the pupil's progress by transferring the strand scores to the photocopiable Record Sheets, which take the form of a bar chart (pages 106–109). The national averages are shown in tints on each bar of the chart, so that you can compare the performance of a child or of the class against them.

Obtaining other scores

Refer to the appropriate tables in this manual to obtain the standardised score, age-standardised score, percentile, reading age, Hodder Scale score and performance indicator for each pupil. You can then enter each pupil's scores on the photocopiable Record Sheets. Alternatively, use MARK to automate the whole score conversion process and to unlock *GaPS'* full performance analysis, diagnostic and predictive potential (see page 26).

In the tables beneath each term's mark scheme we have provided information about pupils' performance in *GaPS* from the standardisation trial. There is also a breakdown of the marks by strand. The mark schemes also include the facility for each question. This shows the percentage success on every question by pupils in the standardisation trial. All this information provides teachers with data to help them investigate a child's results.

In addition, the case studies in Chapter 4 show how teachers have been able to use this information along with standardised scores and the Hodder Scale to inform their teaching. Do be aware though that each of these measurement scales provides independent information and at times there will be differences between them, as they are generated using different methods. When they do give differing information this alerts teachers to investigate further, as it may be that a child has a patchy performance and that this is affecting the analyses.

The performance indicator bands reflect where children, groups, classes and the schools are in relation to other schools term on term. The termly tests sample a broad range of the National Curriculum content for that year, ensuring the child is assessed on an appropriate proportion of the curriculum content.

Using the online analysis and reports

MARK (My Assessment and Reporting Kit) is the powerful online platform that helps teachers to get more from *GaPS* and other assessments by RS Assessment from Hodder Education. To unlock your access to online analysis and reports within MARK go to www.risingstars-uk.com/mark. Detailed user guides and help to get started can be found online at www.rsassessment.com/support.

For customers using the paper tests you can record the marks that your pupils have scored in the *GaPS* tests. This can be done either by importing a CSV file containing their results, or by manually entering their scores via the marksheets.

On the 'Questions' tab you can view the facility value of each question and the average score across all the pupils who are in the class or group – allowing a quick onscreen view of which questions the class as a whole were doing well on or were struggling with.

On the 'Strands' tab, you can see the children's performance in each strand (grammar, punctuation, vocabulary and spelling), allowing a quick overview of how each child is performing by strand.

The Gap Analysis Export allows you to export a CSV with question level marks and a summary of performance at strand and test level.

You can generate a range of reports to analyse the performance of pupils, groups and classes.

- The individual pupil report shows the performance of an individual pupil on their most recently taken test.
- The pupil progress report compares the performance of an individual pupil across a number of tests.
- The intake, class or group report shows the performance of different groups on a specific test.
    - the progress report shows the performance of one group across a number of tests
    - the analysis report shows the performance of one group on a specific test, their average score and the national average standardised score
    - the listing report shows the performance of one group on a specific test, the proportion matching expectations and their average performance by strand.

Answers and mark scheme: GaPS 3 Autumn

Section A: Grammar, punctuation and vocabulary

Question	Answer and marking guidance	Strand reference	Facility %
1	Award **one mark** for all **three** words encircled. (yesterday,) (anisha) went to (bradford) on the bus.	P, G5 G5.1 Capital letters	74
2	Award **one mark** for: (playing)	G, G4 G4.1d Present and past progressive (Year 2), G4.1a Simple past and simple present	89
3	Award **one mark** for: My dad helped me with my homework. ☑	G, G4 G4.1a Simple past and simple present (Year 2)	77
4	Award **one mark** for **all** lines correct. Can I play with you — question What a good idea that is — exclamation We are playing hide and seek — statement Run away and hide — command	G, G2 G2.1 Statements, G2.2 Questions, G2.3 Commands, G2.4 Exclamations	39
5	Award **one mark** for: quickly ☑	G, G1 G1.6 Adverbs	96
6	Award **one mark** for **three** correctly punctuated sentences. What a nasty bruise you have **!** Who did it **?** The boy ran away **.**	P, G5 G5.2 Full stops, G5.3 Question marks, G5.4 Exclamation marks (G, G2.1 Statements, G2.2 Questions, G2.4 Commands)	52
7	Award **one mark** for: Did anyone find a question they couldn't do ☑	P, G5 G5.3 Question marks	71

Question	Answer and marking guidance	Strand reference	Facility %
8	Award **one mark** if the correct contraction, clearly showing the apostrophe between the *u* and the *r*, is written in the gap: **You're** being very kind to me. You should still award the mark if there is no capital letter.	P, G5 G5.8 Apostrophes	49
9	Award **one mark** for: and ☑	G, G3 G3.3 Co-ordinating conjunctions	74
10	Award **one mark** for: full stop ☑	P, G5 G5.2 Full stops	46
11	Award **one mark** for: before ☑	G, G1 G1.4 Conjunctions	70
12	Award **one mark** if **all** adjectives are appropriately constructed and correctly spelled. | Adjective	er	est
---	---	---
tall	taller	tallest
sad	**sadder**	saddest
happy	happier	**happiest**		V, G6 G6.3 Suffixes	24
13	Award **one mark** for: Is it a fact that all racing cars are very fast? Both word order and punctuation must be correct for the mark to be awarded. Ignore minor copying errors.	G, G2 G2.2 Questions	19
14	Award **one mark** for: huge ☑	G, G3 G3.2 Noun phrases	53
15	Award **one mark** for **both** correct. Jax enjoyed his cheese tomato egg and ketchup sandwiches. (ticks on 3rd and 4th arrows)	P, G5 G5.5 Commas in lists	62
16	Award **one mark** for **all** lines correct. Prefix — Word super — freeze anti — hero auto — graph If more than one line is drawn to a box, the mark should not be awarded.	V, G6 G6.2 Prefixes	65

Question	Answer and marking guidance	Strand reference	Facility %
17	Award **one mark** for **three** correct words. **re**write **dis**belief **mis**understand **Accept** the same prefix being used on more than one occasion, i.e. miswrite, misbelief, misunderstand.	V, G6 G6.2 Prefixes	50
18	Award **one mark** for: Juan likes coffee (but) Camilla prefers hot chocolate.	G,1 G1.4 Conjunctions	61
19	Award **one mark** for **both** correct verb phrases. Mr Patel **was pleased** with us. Everyone **was trying** to win the prize. **Also accept**: Everyone **tried** to win the prize.	G, G4 G4.1a Simple past and simple present	43
20	Award **one mark** if **all four** words in the noun phrase are underlined. The pretty little cat can jump up high.	G, G3 G3.2 Noun phrases	10
21	Award **one mark** if the main clause is underlined. Samir asked for popcorn when he went to the cinema.	G, G3 G3.1 Sentences and clauses	13
22	Award **one mark** for: Shall I come tomorrow instead? ☑	P, G5 G5.8 Apostrophes	50
23	Award **one mark** for: "You should have done it before we left the house!" (third arrow ticked)	G, G1 G1.7 Prepositions	51
24	Award **one mark** for **all** correct. | Word	ment	ness
---	---	---
enjoy	✓	
happy		✓
argue	✓	
kind		✓		V, G6 G6.3 Suffixes	79
25	Award **one mark** if the sentence is correctly punctuated. I've told you that you can have a snack of fruit, nuts or vegetables. **All three** must be correct for **one mark**. Also accept a response in which the text has been annotated with the correct punctuation.	P, G5 G5.5 Commas in lists, G5.8 Apostrophes	24

Section B: Spelling

Question	Answer and marking guidance	Strand reference	Facility %
1	Award **one mark** for: The squirrels were **busy** burying their food. The correct spelling of the word **busy**.	S37 Common exception words (Year 2)	57
2	Award **one mark** for: Your **wrist** joins your hand to your arm. The correct spelling of the word **wrist**.	S17 The /r/ sound spelled *wr* at the beginning of words (Year 2)	30
3	Award **one mark** for: The **parents** came to watch the school play. The correct spelling of the word **parents**.	S37 Common exception words (Year 2)	45
4	Award **one mark** for: In spring, the **grass** is green. The correct spelling of the word **grass**.	S37 Common exception words (Year 2)	81
5	Award **one mark** for: I am in red **group** for reading. The correct spelling of the word **group**.	S37 Common exception words	65
6	Award **one mark** for: Think of a **sentence** to describe a cat. The correct spelling of the word **sentence**.	S37 Common exception words	39
7	Award **one mark** for: Hari is too **young** to play with us. The correct spelling of the word **young**.	S40 The /ʌ/ sound spelled *ou*	56
8	Award **one mark** for: We eat **fruit** at snack time. The correct spelling of the word **fruit**.	S37 Common exception words	59
9	Award **one mark** for: Your **heart** pumps your blood round your body. The correct spelling of the word **heart**.	S37 Common exception words	51
10	Award **one mark** for: Did you **learn** your three times table? The correct spelling of the word **learn**.	S37 Common exception words	57
11	Award **one mark** for: Ten is the same as **double** five. The correct spelling of the word **double**.	S40 The /ʌ/ sound spelled *ou*	50
12	Award **one mark** for: My sister gave me a **quarter** of her cake. The correct spelling of the word **quarter**.	S37 Common exception words	26

Answers and mark scheme: *GaPS 3 Autumn*

Question	Answer and marking guidance	Strand reference	Facility %
13	Award **one mark** for: The <u>veins</u> in my arm look blue. The correct spelling of the word **veins**.	S52 Words with the /eɪ/ sound spelled *ei*, *eigh*, or *ey*	9
14	Award **one mark** for: Did you <u>consider</u> all the choices in the question? The correct spelling of the word **consider**.	S37 Common exception words	53
15	Award **one mark** for: A square has four <u>straight</u> sides. The correct spelling of the word **straight**.	S52 Words with the /eɪ/ sound spelled *ei*, *eigh*, or *ey*	22
16	Award **one mark** for: Some stories have too many <u>characters</u>. The correct spelling of the word **characters**.	S48 Words with the /k/ sound spelled *ch*	18
17	Award **one mark** for: The little cat's <u>weight</u> was a surprise. The correct spelling of the word **weight**.	S37 Common exception words	24
18	Award **one mark** for: I <u>caught</u> the ball and threw it back. The correct spelling of the word **caught**.	S37 Common exception words	29
19	Award **one mark** for: I can make this apple <u>disappear</u>. The correct spelling of the word **disappear**.	S37 Common exception words	19
20	Award **one mark** for: A <u>myth</u> is a kind of story. The correct spelling of the word **myth**.	S39 The /ɪ/ sound spelled *y* other than at the end of words	30

GaPS 3 Autumn: Analysis of performance by strand

Strand	Number of marks available	National average mark	National average %
Grammar	13	6.61	51
Punctuation	8	4.03	50
Vocabulary	4	1.97	49
Spelling	20	8.10	40
Total	**45**	**20.71**	**46**

Facility range and number of questions

Facility range	Number of questions at this facility
90–100%	1
60–89%	12
20–59%	26
0–19%	6

Answers and mark scheme: GaPS 3 Spring

Section A: Grammar, punctuation and vocabulary

Question	Answer and marking guidance	Strand reference	Facility %
1	Award **one mark** for: (likes)	G, G4 G4.1a Simple past and simple present	89
2	Award **one mark** for **three** correctly punctuated sentences. What fun that race was! I had fun doing that race. Was that race fun for you?	P, G5 G5.2 Full stops, G5.3 Question marks, G5.4 Exclamation marks	59
3	Award **one mark** for **both** answers correct. | Adjective	Suffix er	Suffix est
---	---	---
late	later	latest
early	earlier	**earliest**
big	**bigger**	biggest		G, G1 G1.3 Adjectives	46
4	Award **one mark** for: "Carli, can you do a wheelie on your bike?" asked Sammi. ☑	P, G5 G5.7 Inverted commas	77
5	Award **one mark** for **both** answers correct. An adjective: __new__ A verb: __helps **or** (to) write__	G, G1 G1.2 Verbs, G1.3 Adjectives	25
6	Award **one mark** for: comma ☑	P, G5 G5.5 Commas in lists	72
7	Award **one mark** for all **three** correct. **a** banana **a** carrot **an** egg	G, G7 G7.1 Standard English	78
8	Award **one mark** for: **Has he** got all my favourite DVDs? Both word order and punctuation must be correct for the mark to be awarded.	G, G2 G2.2 Questions	38

Question	Answer and marking guidance	Strand reference	Facility %
9	Award **one mark** for **both** correct. In our garden, we have planted potato [potatoes] [strawberries] and strawberry. The plurals must be correctly spelled for the mark to be awarded.	V, G6 G6.3 Suffixes	11
10	Award **one mark** for: (when)	G, G1 G1.4 Conjunctions	79
11	Award **one** mark for **both** correct. I can make a paper plain / (plane.) Put your coat down hear/ (here.)	V, G6 G6.5 Homophones and near-homophones	72
12	Award **one mark** for **both** correct. ↑ I would ↑ like some more, ↑ said ↑ Dad. ↑ ✓ ✓	P, G5 G5.7 Inverted commas	57
13	Award **one mark** for **three** correct nouns. 	Word	Noun
---	---
relax	relax**ation**
enjoy	enjoy**ment**
kind	kind**ness**
inform	inform**ation** | **Accept** suffixes written without the root word: ment, ness, ation.	V, G6 G6.3 Suffixes	51
14	Award **one mark** for all **three** correct. (did) you know that (julian) went to (france) in the holidays?	P, G5 G5.1 Capital letters	70
15	Award **one mark** for **both** words spelled correctly. | Verb	ing	ed
---	---	---
paint	painting	painted
smile	**smiling**	smiled
carry	carrying	**carried**		G, G1 G1.2 Verbs	31

Answers and mark scheme: *GaPS 3 Spring*   33

Question	Answer and marking guidance	Strand reference	Facility %
16	Award **one mark** for: has been ☑ **Also accept**: is going ☑	G, G4 G4.1a Simple past and simple present	42
17	Award **one mark** for **both** apostrophes correct. I'd like to see Alberto's new trainers.	P, G5 G5.8 Apostrophes	43
18	Award **one mark** for: new ☑	G, G3 G3.2 Noun phrases	38
19	Award **one mark** for **both** answers correct. 	Singular noun	Plural noun
---	---
orange	oranges
cherry	**cherries**
peach	**peaches** | Words must be spelled correctly for the mark to be awarded.	V, G6 G6.3 Suffixes	29
20	Award **one mark** for: or	G, G3 G3.1 Sentences and clauses	88
21	Award **one mark** for **both** responses correct. Our sunflowers have **grown** a lot this year. Shall we **meet** at the station on Sunday?	V, G6 G6.5 Homophones and near-homophones	55
22	Award **one mark** for **three** correct punctuation marks. "Can we take Lee's bike to the park, if he's good?	P, G5 G5.8 Apostrophes, G5.7 Inverted commas	29
23	Award **one mark** for **all** lines correct. have done — ate has eaten — did has gone — saw have seen — went	G, G4 G4.1b Verbs in the perfect form	91

Question	Answer and marking guidance	Strand reference	Facility %
24	Award **one** mark for all **three** correct. My dad said he would take me swimming **but** he couldn't find his kit. Would you like eggs for breakfast **or** would you prefer cereal? I like reading **and** I like writing too.	G, G3 G3.3 Co-ordinating conjunctions	82
25	Award **one** mark for **all** correct. 		Full stop	Exclamation mark	Question mark
Can you tell the time			✓
What a clever dog that is		✓	
The rabbit is fast asleep	✓		
What will happen next			✓		P, G5 G5.2 Full stops, G5.3 Question marks, G5.4 Exclamation marks	50

Section B: Spelling

Question	Answer and marking guidance	Strand reference	Facility %
1	Award **one** mark for: The **biggest** is not always the best. The correct spelling of the word **biggest**.	S38 Adding suffixes beginning with vowel letters to words of more than one syllable	67
2	Award **one** mark for: The fire was burning in the **grate**. The correct spelling of the word **grate**.	S61 Homophones and near-homophones	52
3	Award **one** mark for: What did you **decide**? The correct spelling of the word **decide**.	S37 Common exception words	41
4	Award **one** mark for: Tell me what you **thought**. The correct spelling of the word **thought**.	S37 Common exception words	54
5	Award **one** mark for: Can you **hear** me? The correct spelling of the word **hear**.	S61 Homophones and near-homophones	78

Answers and mark scheme: *GaPS 3 Spring*

Question	Answer and marking guidance	Strand reference	Facility %
6	Award **one mark** for: Ayla <u>gently</u> stroked the kitten. The correct spelling of the word **gently**.	S43 The suffix –ly	57
7	Award **one mark** for: The <u>happiest</u> person won a prize. The correct spelling of the word **happiest**.	S24 Adding –ed, –ing, –er and –est to a root word ending in y with a consonant before it	51
8	Award **one mark** for: Can you <u>remember</u> your phone number? The correct spelling of the word **remember**.	S37 Common exception words	60
9	Award **one mark** for: My grandad grew the <u>heaviest</u> pumpkin. The correct spelling of the word **heaviest**.	S24 Adding –ed, –ing, –er and –est to a root word ending in y with a consonant before it	28
10	Award **one mark** for: It is always <u>possible</u> to learn. The correct spelling of the word **possible**.	S37 Common exception words	39
11	Award **one mark** for: The train went <u>through</u> the tunnel. The correct spelling of the word **through**.	S37 Common exception words	48
12	Award **one mark** for: Do you live near a sports <u>centre</u>? The correct spelling of the word **centre**.	S37 Common exception words	29
13	Award **one mark** for: We are making <u>decorations</u> for the school. The correct spelling of the word **decorations**.	S47 Endings that sound like /ʃən/, spelled –tion, –sion, –ssion, –cian	31
14	Award **one mark** for: Hit the ball <u>forwards</u> to your partner. The correct spelling of the word **forwards**.	S37 Common exception words	44
15	Award **one mark** for: Your <u>height</u> means how tall you are. The correct spelling of the word **height**.	S37 Common exception words	25
16	Award **one mark** for: Listen carefully to the <u>information</u>. The correct spelling of the word **information**.	S42 The suffix –ation	53

Question	Answer and marking guidance	Strand reference	Facility %
17	Award **one mark** for: People who are <u>popular</u> have lots of friends. The correct spelling of the word **popular**.	S37 Common exception words	48
18	Award **one mark** for: It is easy to grow <u>tomatoes</u>. The correct spelling of the word **tomatoes**.	S5 Adding –s and –es to words (plural of nouns and the third-person singular of verbs)	26
19	Award **one mark** for: You need to take <u>particular</u> care today. The correct spelling of the word **particular**.	S37 Common exception words	25
20	Award **one mark** for: I will eat rice <u>although</u> I prefer pasta. The correct spelling of the word **although**.	S59 Words containing the letter string *ough*	38

GaPS 3 Spring: Analysis of performance by strand

Strand	Number of marks available	National average mark	National average %
Grammar	12	7.05	59
Punctuation	8	4.34	54
Vocabulary	5	2.11	42
Spelling	20	8.86	44
Total	45	22.35	50

Facility range and number of questions

Facility range	Number of questions at this facility
90–100%	1
60–89%	12
20–59%	31
0–19%	1

Answers and mark scheme: *GaPS 3 Summer*

Section A: Grammar, punctuation and vocabulary

Question	Answer and marking guidance	Strand reference	Facility %
1	Award **one mark** for: (learned)	G, G4 G4.1a Simple past and simple present (G1.2 Verbs)	91
2	Award **one mark** for all **three** correct. I really like the story you wrote. What a wonderful story you wrote**!** Was that the best story you have written**?**	P, G5 G5.2 Full stops, G5.3 Question marks, G5.4 Exclamation marks	71
3	Award **one mark** for all **three** correct. The mother giraffe is tall**er** than her baby. The sun is hot**ter** in the morning than it is in the evening. The fast**est** lions go hunting. The adjectives must be correctly spelled for the mark to be awarded.	V, G6 G6.3 Suffixes	34
4	Award **one mark** for: You have finished your work. Both word order and punctuation must be correct for the mark to be awarded.	G, G2 G2.2 Questions (G, G2.1 Statements, P, G5.3 Question marks)	48
5	Award **one mark** for: Listen to the teacher. **Also accept**: Listen to the teacher!	G, G2 G2.3 Commands	60
6	Award **one mark** for: I like watching cartoons (when) they make me laugh.	G, G3 G3.4 Subordinating conjunctions and subordinate clauses	62

Question	Answer and marking guidance	Strand reference	Facility %
7	Award **one mark** for **both** correct. +un **unhappy** +ness **happiness** happy +ly **happily** +un and +ly **unhappily** Both words must be spelled correctly for the mark to be awarded.	V, G6 G6.4 Word families (G6.2 Prefixes, G6.3 Suffixes)	49
8	Award **one mark** for **both** inverted commas correctly placed. "Will you help me to bake a cake?" asked Dad. **Accept** single or double inverted commas.	P, G5 G5.7 Inverted commas	67
9	Award **one mark** for a corrected completed table. | Sentence	Past tense	Present tense
---	---	---
We are working hard.		✓
We worked hard.	✓	
In our class we work hard.		✓
He has worked hard.	✓			G, G4 G4.1 Verb forms	36
10	Award **one mark** for **all** lines correct. A B act — enjoy heal — healer joy — prescription scribe — reaction **Accept** other methods of identifying the correct answer.	V, G6 G6.4 Word families	88
11	Award **one mark** for: You're all invited to my party. ☑	P, G5 G5.8 Apostrophes	56

Question	Answer and marking guidance	Strand reference	Facility %
12	Award **one** mark for **both** correct. Wiktoria dived into the deep end of the pool. ↑ V ↑ A ↑ N	G, G1 G1.1 Nouns, G1.2 Verbs, G1.3 Adjectives	78
13	Award **one** mark for: Look how fast that rabbit is running! That rabbit can run very fast!	P, G5 G5.4 Exclamation marks	38
14	Award **one** mark for **both** apostrophes correctly placed. "We can't see," complained Jane's little sisters.	P, G5 G5.8 Apostrophes	31
15	Award **one** mark for: What a lot of doughnuts you ate ☑	G, G2 G2.4 Exclamations	52
16	Award **one** mark for either: The colourful fish swam through the seaweed. **OR** The fish swam through the colourful seaweed. Capital letter and full stop do not have to be correct for the mark to be awarded. **Also accept**: colourful fish, colourful seaweed. Ignore minor copying errors.	G, G3 G3.2 Noun phrases	34
17	Award **one** mark for: (So)	G, G3 G3.4 Subordinating conjunctions and subordinate clauses	79
18	Award **one** mark for **both** correct. Did you know that (kangaroos) live in (Australia)?	G, G1 G1.1 Nouns	82
19	Award **one** mark for all **three** correct. you're don't they'll	P, G5 G5.8 Apostrophes	71
20	Award **one** mark for: because we do fun things. ☑	G, G3 G3.4 Subordinating conjunctions and subordinate clauses	77

Answers and mark scheme: *GaPS 3 Summer*

Question	Answer and marking guidance	Strand reference	Facility %
21	Award **one mark** for all correct. Prefixes: dis, mis, re, un Verbs: courage, do, lead, turn dis — courage mis — lead re — turn un — do	V, G6 G6.2 Prefixes	39
22	Award **one mark** for When Imran climbs, he seems to be <u>fearless</u>.	V, G6 G6.3 Suffixes	33
23	Award **one mark** for all three correct. David asked, "Would you like lemon jam, or butter on your pancakes?"	P, G5 G5.7 Inverted commas	30
24	Award **one mark** for: A man walked on the moon. ☑	G, G4 G4.1b Verbs in the perfect form	66
25	Award **one** mark for: Shall we play with Lego <u>or</u> play a board game? I prefer Lego <u>but</u> there's not much left in the box. Why don't we go to another class <u>and</u> ask if we can borrow some Lego?	G, G3 G3.3 Co-ordinating conjunctions	75

Section B: Spelling

Question	Answer and marking guidance	Strand reference	Facility %
1	Award **one mark** for: <u>Thursday</u> is my favourite day. The correct spelling of the word **Thursday**.	S37 Common exception words	80
2	Award **one mark** for: My <u>address</u> tells people where I live. The correct spelling of the word **address**.	S37 Common exception words	49
3	Award **one mark** for: We <u>usually</u> go swimming on Mondays. The correct spelling of the word **usually**.	S43 The suffix –ly	22
4	Award **one mark** for: How would you <u>describe</u> yourself? The correct spelling of the word **describe**.	S37 Common exception words	58

Answers and mark scheme: *GaPS 3 Summer*

Question	Answer and marking guidance	Strand reference	Facility %
5	Award **one mark** for: I like peanut butter <u>although</u> I don't like peanuts. The correct spelling of the word **although**.	S37 Common exception words	45
6	Award **one mark** for: You <u>appear</u> to be very happy at school. The correct spelling of the word **appear**.	S37 Common exception words	58
7	Award **one mark** for: Which <u>particular</u> puppy do you like best? The correct spelling of the word **particular**.	S37 Common exception words	29
8	Award **one mark** for: We did an <u>investigation</u> in science. The correct spelling of the word **investigation**.	S42 The suffix –*ation*	43
9	Award **one mark** for: We will have a break once we <u>complete</u> this assessment. The correct spelling of the word **complete**.	S37 Common exception words	56
10	Award **one mark** for: Lola <u>misheard</u> what the teacher said. The correct spelling of the word **misheard**.	S41 Prefixes	45
11	Award **one mark** for: Simon had to <u>rewrite</u> his messy work. The correct spelling of the word **rewrite**.	S41 Prefixes	65
12	Award **one mark** for: The month after January is <u>February</u>. The correct spelling of the word **February**. February must be spelled with a capital F for the mark to be awarded.	S37 Common exception words	37
13	Award **one mark** for: <u>Perhaps</u> we should take our umbrellas with us today. The correct spelling of the word **perhaps**. The capital letter is not necessary for the mark to be awarded.	S37 Common exception words	55
14	Award **one mark** for: Will you let me know when they <u>arrive</u>? The correct spelling of the word **arrive**.	S37 Common exception words	50
15	Award **one mark** for: He is <u>actually</u> getting a quad bike. The correct spelling of the word **actually**.	S37 Common exception words	30

Question	Answer and marking guidance	Strand reference	Facility %
16	Award **one mark** for: Do you think that will be <u>impossible</u>? The correct spelling of the word **impossible**.	S41 Prefixes	34
17	Award **one mark** for: Artur liked the <u>scene</u> when the pirates came on stage. The correct spelling of the word **scene**.	S61 Homophones and near-homophones	33
18	Award **one mark** for: For <u>relaxation</u>, he loved to read. The correct spelling of the word **relaxation**.	S42 The suffix –ation	40
19	Award **one mark** for: Luke had a <u>disagreement</u> with his best friend. The correct spelling of the word **disagreement**.	S41 Prefixes	40
20	Award **one mark** for: If I work hard at anything, I will <u>improve</u>. The correct spelling of the word **improve**.	S41 Prefixes	64

GaPS 3 Summer: Analysis of performance by strand

Strand	Number of marks available	National average mark	National average %
Grammar	13	8.15	63
Punctuation	7	3.74	53
Vocabulary	5	2.41	48
Spelling	20	9.24	46
Total	45	23.54	52

Facility range and number of questions

Facility range	Number of questions at this facility
90–100%	1
60–89%	15
20–59%	29
0–19%	0

Answers and mark scheme: GaPS 4 Autumn

Section A: Grammar, punctuation and vocabulary

Question	Answer and marking guidance	Strand reference	Facility %
1	Award **one mark** for: verb ☑	G, G1 G1.2 Verbs	38
2	Award **one mark** for all **three** correct words circled: (I) know that (madrid) is the capital city of (spain.)	P, G5 G5.1 Capital letters	70
3	Award **one mark** for **all** lines correct. What are — we meet? When do — they doing? Who will — they start? Why are — we going?	G, G2 G2.2 Questions	85
4	Award **one mark** for all **three** correct. aware**ness** hope**ful** pain**ful** **Accept** incorrect spellings of the suffix.	V, G6 G6.3 Suffixes	74
5	Award **one mark** for **all** lines correct. Do you like working on the computer — ? What a fantastic model you have made — ! You need to sit quietly on the carpet — .	P, G5 G5.3 Question marks	58
6	Award **one mark** for: adverb ☑	G, G1 G1 Grammatical terms/word classes	46
7	Award **one mark** for **both** commas correct. You need flour**,** sugar**,** eggs and butter to make a cake.	P, G5 G5.5 Commas in lists	78
8	Award **one mark** for: the high hill ☑	G, G3 G3.2 Noun phrases	34

Question	Answer and marking guidance	Strand reference	Facility %
9	Award **one mark** for: send	G, G4 G4.2 Tense consistency	54
10	Award **one mark** for: Alex's baby **Do not accept** Alexs' baby. For the mark to be awarded, the apostrophe must clearly be between the *x* and the *s*.	P, G5 G5.8 Apostrophes	70
11	Award **one mark** for **all** lines correct. **Word** **Suffix** enjoy — ment joy — ful relax — ation	V, G6 G6.3 Suffixes	81
12	Award **one mark** for **all** correct. | Word	super	sub
---	---	---
heading		✓
market	✓	
way		✓		V, G6 G6.2 Prefixes	81
13	Award **one mark** for: Scientists **discover** new things each day. **Also accept** discovered, are discovering, were discovering, will be discovering, have been discovering.	V, G6 G6.4 Word families	52
14	Award **one mark** for **all** correct. | Present tense	Simple past	Present perfect tense
---	---	---
is playing	played	has played
are walking	walked	have walked	 **Do not accept** has walked.	G, G4 G4.1b Verbs in the perfect form	13
15	Award **one mark** for: Trudy draws beautiful pictures, **although** she finds it tiring.	G, G3 G3.4 Subordinating conjunctions and subordinate clauses	78

Question	Answer and marking guidance	Strand reference	Facility %
16	Award **one mark** for: <u>When we went to the park</u>, we saw some builders digging the road. **Accept** answers when the comma is underlined (and when it is not). **Also accept** <u>When we went</u>	G, G1 G1.6a Adverbials	30
17	Award **one mark** for: Ben was feeling very happy. ☑	G, G7 G7.1 Standard English	71
18	Award **one mark** for: "Stand by the door," said Mrs Green. **Both** opening and closing inverted commas need to be present for the mark to be awarded. The closing set of inverted commas need to be clearly after the comma for the mark to be awarded.	P, G5 G5.7 Inverted commas	52
19	Award **one mark** for: he ☑	G, G1 G1.5 Pronouns	88
20	Award **one mark** for: Put your shoes on ☑	G, G2 G2.3 Commands	79
21	Award **one mark** for: <u>What a loud noise you made!</u> The exclamation mark and capital letter need to be present for the mark to be awarded. Ignore minor copying errors.	G, G2 G2.4 Exclamations	28
22	Award **one mark** for: apostrophe ☑	P, G5 G5.8 Apostrophes	55
23	Award **one mark** for: <u>they're</u>	P, G5 G5.8 Apostrophes	42
24	Award **one mark** for: The glass was **empty**.	G, G1 G1.3 Adjectives	44
25	Award **one mark** for: Ali washed her hands **before** making lunch. **Also accept** other possible correct answers. Indicative answers could be: after, when, while.	G, G1 G1.4 Conjunctions	60

Answers and mark scheme: *GaPS 4 Autumn*

Section B: Spelling

Question	Answer and marking guidance	Strand reference	Facility %
1	Award **one mark** for: Shania hopped **slowly** on one leg. The correct spelling of the word **slowly**.	S43 The suffix –*ly* (Year 3)	82
2	Award **one mark** for: The school is closed in **August**. The correct spelling of the word **August**. August must be spelled with a capital A for the mark to be awarded.	S37 Common exception words (Year 3)	45
3	Award **one mark** for: The glove was **smaller** than his hand. The correct spelling of the word **smaller**.	S7 Adding –*er* and –*est* to adjectives where no change is needed in the root word (Year 3)	80
4	Award **one mark** for: It is **important** to brush your teeth. The correct spelling of the word **important**.	S37 Common exception words	61
5	Award **one mark** for: An old-fashioned word for a car is **automobile**. The correct spelling of the word **automobile**.	S41 Prefixes	34
6	Award **one mark** for: The volcano had been **inactive** for hundreds of years. The correct spelling of the word **inactive**.	S41 Prefixes	73
7	Award **one mark** for: Joshua was **impolite** to his teacher. The correct spelling of the word **impolite**.	S41 Prefixes	43
8	Award **one mark** for: I would like to invent a brand new **machine**. The correct spelling of the word **machine**.	S49 Words with the /ʃ/ sound spelled *ch*	57
9	Award **one mark** for: Efe's colourful outfit for the carnival was **unique**. The correct spelling of the word **unique**.	S50 Words ending with the /g/ sound spelled –*gue* and the /k/ sound spelled –*que*	24
10	Award **one mark** for: You can **build** a tower of bricks. The correct spelling of the word **build**.	S37 Common exception words	72

Answers and mark scheme: *GaPS 4 Autumn*

Question	Answer and marking guidance	Strand reference	Facility %
11	Award **one mark** for: That story is hard to **believe**. The correct spelling of the word **believe**.	S37 Common exception words	20
12	Award **one mark** for: On a cold day, I love to **imagine** it is summer. The correct spelling of the word **imagine**.	S37 Common exception words	43
13	Award **one mark** for: My favourite month is **November**. The correct spelling of the word **November**. **Do not accept** a reverse letter 'N'	S37 Common exception words (Year 3)	84
14	Award **one mark** for: It was so cold I could see my **breath**. The correct spelling of the word **breath**.	S37 Common exception words	71
15	Award **one mark** for: The **chef** cooked a wonderful meal. The correct spelling of the word **chef**.	S49 Words with the /ʃ/ sound spelled *ch*	61
16	Award **one mark** for: All the children stood in a **circle**. The correct spelling of the word **circle**.	S37 Common exception words (Year 3)	71
17	Award **one mark** for: You see an **increase** in the number of butterflies in the summer. The correct spelling of the word **increase**.	S37 Common exception words	47
18	Award **one mark** for: Edward found it **strange** that Mr Green always wore a hat. The correct spelling of the word **strange**.	S37 Common exception words	71
19	Award **one mark** for: The teacher said to cut carefully with your **scissors**. The correct spelling of the word **scissors**.	S51 Words with the /s/ sound spelled *sc*	25
20	Award **one mark** for: Some people can use the stars as a **guide** to find their way. The correct spelling of the word **guide**.	S37 Common exception words	49

GaPS 4 Autumn: Analysis of performance by strand

Strand	Number of marks available	National average mark	National average %
Grammar	14	7.15	51
Punctuation	7	4.00	57
Vocabulary	4	2.78	70
Spelling	20	10.47	52
Total	**45**	**24.40**	**54**

Facility range and number of questions

Facility range	Number of questions at this facility
90–100%	0
60–89%	22
20–59%	22
0–19%	1

Answers and mark scheme: GaPS 4 Spring

Section A: Grammar, punctuation and vocabulary

Question	Answer and marking guidance	Strand reference	Facility %
1	Award **one mark** for: adverb ☑	G, G1 G1 Grammatical terms/word classes	61
2	Award **one mark** for: the girl's shoes ☑	G, G3, G1 G3.2 Noun phrases, G1.3 Adjectives	75
3	Award **one mark** for: put your pens down or Put your pens down. **OR** put down your pens or Put down your pens.	G, G2 G2.3 Commands	82
4	Award **one mark** for all **three** words correctly encircled. (harry) and (milly) wanted to visit (africa) to see the wildlife.	P, G5 G5.1 Capital letters	92
5	Award **one mark** for **three** correct words. neighbour**hood** sportsman**ship** friend**ship**	V, G6 G6.3 Suffixes	82
6	Award **one mark** for **three** correct answers. The children — **are playing.** The cat — **is washing.** The ladies — **are working.**	G, G4 G4.2 Tense consistency	87
7	Award **one mark** for: singing ☑	G, G1 G1.2 Verbs	78

Question	Answer and marking guidance	Strand reference	Facility %
8	Award **one mark** for **all** lines correct. inform — ful hope — ation treat — ment (inform→ation, hope→ful, treat→ment)	V, G6 G6.3 Suffixes	86
9	Award **one mark** for **both** correct. Eva **missed** the bus. The **mist** was coming in from the sea.	V, G6 G6.5 Homophones and near-homophones	95
10	Award **one mark** for: They did the spelling test first. ☑	G, G7 G7.1 Standard English	87
11	Award **one mark** for: "Would you like to come and play at my house?" asked Jamil. Both opening and closing inverted commas need to be present for the mark to be awarded. The closing set of inverted commas needs to be clearly after the question mark for the mark to be awarded.	P, G5 G5.7 Inverted commas	67
12	Award **one mark** for: the children's garden The apostrophe needs to be clearly between the n and the s for the mark to be awarded.	P, G5 G5.8 Apostrophes	66
13	Award **one mark** for: **thinks**	G, G4 G4.2 Tense consistency	33
14	Award **one mark** for: **trans**form **Also accept** other possible correct answers. Indicative answers could be: biform, deform, inform, uniform and triform.	V, G6 G6.2 Prefixes	68
15	Award **one mark** for **both** correct. The teacher was looking forward to having a **break**. The rider had to **brake** down the steep hill.	V, G6 G6.5 Homophones and near-homophones	54
16	Award **one mark** for: Is Tom thirstier than Ben? **Also accept**: Is Ben thirstier than Tom? The question mark should be present for the mark to be awarded. Accept minor copying errors. There is no need for inverted commas to be present for the mark to be awarded.	P, G5 G5.1 Capital letters, G5.2 Full stops, G5.3 Question marks (G, G2 G2.2 Questions)	61

Answers and mark scheme: *GaPS 4 Spring*

Question	Answer and marking guidance	Strand reference	Facility %
17	Award **one mark** for: "Look! My sunflower is starting to grow!" said Owen excitedly. Both opening and closing inverted commas need to be present for the mark to be awarded. The closing set of inverted commas needs to be clearly after the exclamation mark for the mark to be awarded.	P, G5 G5.7 Inverted commas	85
18	Award **one mark** for: birds ☑	G, G1 G1.5 Pronouns	45
19	Award **one mark** for: What a messy room this is ☑	G, G2 G2.4 Exclamations	54
20	Award **one mark** for: Outside in the playground, there was excitement about the new climbing frame. (comma after "playground" marked ✓)	P, G5 G5.6b Commas after fronted adverbials	68
21	Award **one mark** for: We have to wash our clothes **because** they are dirty. **Also accept** other possible correct answers. Indicative answers could be: when, if, after, as.	G, G1 G1.4 Conjunctions	57
22	Award **one mark** for: a pair of red shoes ☑	G, G3 G3.2 Noun phrases	84
23	Award **one mark** for: during **Accept** minor copying errors.	G, G1 G1.7 Prepositions	79
24	Award **one mark** for: Sam plays football, **before he goes to the swimming pool**. The full stop may or may not be underlined for the mark to be awarded.	G, G3 G3.4 Subordinating conjunctions and subordinate clauses	36
25	Award **one mark** for: more than one boy, more than one umbrella ☑	P, G5 G5.8 Apostrophes	37

Section B: Spelling

Question	Answer and marking guidance	Strand reference	Facility %
1	Award **one mark** for: Sabrina <u>often</u> visits the library. The correct spelling of the word **often**.	S37 Common exception words	81
2	Award **one mark** for: The story in the newspaper had a funny <u>subheading</u>. The correct spelling of the word **subheading**.	S41 Prefixes	74
3	Award **one mark** for: The crowd was waiting to see the <u>superstar</u>. The correct spelling of the word **superstar**.	S41 Prefixes	80
4	Award **one mark** for: The train's <u>destination</u> is Manchester. The correct spelling of the word **destination**.	S47 Endings that sound like /ʃən/ spelled –tion, –sion, –ssion, –cian	51
5	Award **one mark** for: It would be my <u>pleasure</u> to help you. The correct spelling of the word **pleasure**.	S44 Words with endings sounding like /ʒə/ or /tʃə/	49
6	Award **one mark** for: "We never <u>misbehave</u>," said the twins. The correct spelling of the word **misbehave**.	S41 Prefixes	55
7	Award **one mark** for: My sister loves animals and everything to do with <u>nature</u>. The correct spelling of the word **nature**.	S37 Common exception words	73
8	Award **one mark** for: Zak made a <u>picture</u> out of pasta. The correct spelling of the word **picture**.	S44 Words with endings sounding like /ʒə/ or /tʃə/	76
9	Award **one mark** for: I love to grow plants, and <u>therefore</u> I will buy some seeds. The correct spelling of the word **therefore**.	S37 Common exception words	53
10	Award **one mark** for: In Japan, there is an <u>island</u> where only rabbits live. The correct spelling of the word **island**.	S37 Common exception words	76
11	Award **one mark** for: People say eating carrots helps your <u>vision</u>. The correct spelling of the word **vision**.	S45 Endings that sound like /ʒən/	66

Question	Answer and marking guidance	Strand reference	Facility %
12	Award **one mark** for: It can be hard to keep a **promise**. The correct spelling of the word **promise**.	S37 Common exception words	72
13	Award **one mark** for: The wrong ticket caused **confusion**. The correct spelling of the word **confusion**.	S45 Endings that sound like /ʒən/	59
14	Award **one mark** for: Early in the morning, I love the **peace** and quiet. The correct spelling of the word **peace**.	S61 Homophones or near-homophones	72
15	Award **one mark** for: Hanni and Stefan pretended their stones were **treasure**. The correct spelling of the word **treasure**.	S44 Words with endings sounding like /ʒə/ or /tʃə/	61
16	Award **one mark** for: The astronauts were sent on a **mission** to the moon. The correct spelling of the word **mission**.	S47 Endings that sound like /ʃən/ spelled –tion, –sion, –ssion, –cian	53
17	Award **one mark** for: Class 4B did an **experiment** about forces. The correct spelling of the word **experiment**.	S37 Common exception words	47
18	Award **one mark** for: Silk is a delicate **material**. The correct spelling of the word **material**.	S37 Common exception words	36
19	Award **one mark** for: The animals were moved to a larger **enclosure**. The correct spelling of the word **enclosure**.	S44 Words with endings sounding like /ʒə/ or /tʃə/	34
20	Award **one mark** for: My father is a teacher and my mother is a **musician**. The correct spelling of the word **musician**.	S47 Endings that sound like /ʃən/ spelled –tion, –sion, –ssion, –cian	26

GaPS 4 Spring: Analysis of performance by strand

Strand	Number of marks available	National average mark	National average %
Grammar	13	8.43	65
Punctuation	7	4.23	60
Vocabulary	5	4.04	81
Spelling	20	11.91	60
Total	**45**	**28.60**	**64**

Facility range and number of questions

Facility range	Number of questions at this facility
90–100%	0
60–89%	26
20–59%	17
0–19%	0

Answers and mark scheme: GaPS 4 Summer

Section A: Grammar, punctuation and vocabulary

Question	Answer and marking guidance	Strand reference	Facility %
1	Award **one mark** for: After his journey from (manchester) to (london), (ken) was tired.	P, G5 G5.1 Capital letters	82
2	Award **one mark** for: (brought)	G, G4 G4.2 Tense consistency	92
3	Award **one mark** for: The ancient building was crumbling (and) people did not know if they could rebuild it.	G, G3 G3.3 Co-ordinating conjunctions, G3.4 Subordinating conjunctions and subordinate clauses	66
4	Award **one mark** for all **four** lines correct. we are — we're we have — we've we will not — we won't we will — we'll	P, G5 G5.8 Apostrophes	88
5	Award **one mark** for: **took**	G, G4 G4.2 Tense consistency	69
6	Award **one mark** for both inverted commas correctly placed. "You have worked hard. You deserve a treat," said Dad. The closing set of inverted commas needs to be clearly after the comma for the mark to be awarded.	P, G5 G5.7 Inverted commas	57
7	Award **one mark** for: drawing ☑	G, G1 G1.2 Verbs	60

Question	Answer and marking guidance	Strand reference	Facility %
8	Award **one mark** for both correct. bananas ☑ mangoes ☑	G, G1 G1.1 Nouns	87
9	Award **one mark** for: Every year millions of people <u>celebrate</u> special festivals.	V, G6 G6.4 Word families	67
10	Award **one mark** for: <u>hopeful</u> **Accept** other possible correct answers. Indicative answers could be: hoped, hopefulness. Correct spelling required.	V, G6 G6.4 Word families	61
11	Award **one mark** for: "Please tidy your room," Mum said. The closing set of inverted commas needs to be clearly after the comma for the mark to be awarded.	P, G5 G5.7 Inverted commas	51
12	Award **one mark** for: Sabrine found the joke very **humorous**. **Also accept**: humourless. Correct spelling required.	V, G6 G6.3 Suffixes	43
13	Award **one mark** for both correct. (1) <u>I did</u> and (2) <u>you were</u>	G, G7 G7.1 Standard English	45
14	Award **one mark** for: (even though)	G, G3 G3.3 Co-ordinating conjunctions, G3.4 Subordinating conjunctions and subordinate clauses	74
15	Award **one mark** for: The doorbell rang <u>when I was in the bath.</u> **Accept** whether or not the full stop is underlined.	G, G3 G3.4 Subordinating conjunctions and subordinate clauses	40
16	Award **one mark** for: The alarm rings at seven in the morning. ☑ The children look for their friends. ☑	G, G1 G1.2 Verbs	69
17	Award **one mark** for: comma ☑	P, G5 G5.6b Commas after fronted adverbials	86
18	Award **one mark** for: books ☑	G, G1 G1.5 Pronouns	69

Question	Answer and marking guidance	Strand reference	Facility %
19	Award **one mark** for: Before the explorers set out ↑ they packed 　　　　　　　　　　　　　✓ a map ↑ compass ↑ and food ↑ supplies. 　　✓	P, G5 G5.5 Commas in lists	53
20	Award **one mark** for both correctly circled. There are many different kinds of homes: you could live in ⓐ apartment, a bungalow or ⓐⓝ town house.	G, G1 G1.8 Determiners	42
21	Award **one mark** for: **Verb**　　　　　　　　**Noun** frustrate　　　　　　　frustration complete　　　　　　　completion divide　　　　　　　　division All answers must be spelled correctly for the mark to be awarded.	V, G6 G6.3 Suffixes	12
22	Award **one mark** for: they should not	P, G5 G5.8 Apostrophes	73
23	Award **one mark** for all **four** lines correct. auto — mobile inter — city sub — title super — sonic	V, G6 G6.2 Prefixes	71
24	Award **one mark** for: When it was time for lunch, Mum switched the computer off. **Accept** whether or not the comma is underlined.	G, G1 G1.6a Adverbials	57
25	Award **one mark** for both correct. The necklace is mine. The garden is theirs.	G, G1 G1.5a Possessive pronouns	56

Answers and mark scheme: *GaPS 4 Summer*

Section B: Spelling

Question	Answer and marking guidance	Strand reference	Facility %
1	Award **one mark** for: Every child in the swimming team won a <u>medal</u>. The correct spelling of the word **medal**.	S61 Homophones and near-homophones	70
2	Award **one mark** for: A <u>revision</u> was made to the school timetable. The correct spelling of the word **revision**.	S45 Endings that sound like /ʒən/	60
3	Award **one mark** for: The explorer discovered a new <u>creature</u>. The correct spelling of the word **creature**.	S44 Words with endings sounding like /ʒə/ or /tʃə/	71
4	Award **one mark** for: The player hit the ball without <u>hesitation</u>. The correct spelling of the word **hesitation**.	S47 Endings that sound like /ʃən/ spelled –tion, –sion, –ssion, –cian	46
5	Award **one mark** for: Paula lost <u>interest</u> in the game. The correct spelling of the word **interest**.	S37 Common exception words	45
6	Award **one mark** for: Don't go too close to the edge, it's <u>dangerous</u>. The correct spelling of the word **dangerous**.	S46 The suffix –ous	61
7	Award **one mark** for: We measured the <u>length</u> of the playground. The correct spelling of the word **length**.	S37 Common exception words	63
8	Award **one mark** for: Chris was very happy as the holidays were <u>finally</u> here. The correct spelling of the word **finally**.	S43 The suffix –ly	61
9	Award **one mark** for: An <u>enormous</u> crowd had gathered to see the performer. The correct spelling of the word **enormous**.	S46 The suffix –ous	47
10	Award **one mark** for: Morgan kept <u>forgetting</u> to post his friend's birthday card. The correct spelling of the word **forgetting**.	S38 Adding suffixes beginning with vowel letters to words of more than one syllable	41

Question	Answer and marking guidance	Strand reference	Facility %
11	Award **one mark** for: The pet shop was on the **opposite** side of the road. The correct spelling of the word **opposite**.	S37 Common exception words	38
12	Award **one mark** for: Toadstools are often **poisonous**. The correct spelling of the word **poisonous**.	S46 The suffix –*ous*	28
13	Award **one mark** for: The engineer tested the **strength** of the bridge. The correct spelling of the word **strength**.	S37 Common exception words	59
14	Award **one mark** for: "These two chemicals **interact** and change colour," said the teacher. The correct spelling of the word **interact**.	S41 Prefixes	69
15	Award **one mark** for: The school play was a special **occasion**. The correct spelling of the word **occasion**.	S37 Common exception words	36
16	Award **one mark** for: The cover made the book look very **ordinary**. The correct spelling of the word **ordinary**.	S37 Common exception words	49
17	Award **one mark** for: Alma was sure her brother hid her book on **purpose**. The correct spelling of the word **purpose**.	S37 Common exception words	42
18	Award **one mark** for: The shops were very **different** from how she remembered them. The correct spelling of the word **different**.	S37 Common exception words	59
19	Award **one mark** for: Snap was still one of Sam's **favourite** games. The correct spelling of the word **favourite**.	S37 Common exception words	41
20	Award **one mark** for: The weather forecast was **incorrect**. The correct spelling of the word **incorrect**.	S41 Prefixes	63

GaPS 4 Summer: Analysis of performance by strand

Strand	Number of marks available	National average mark	National average %
Grammar	13	8.16	63
Punctuation	7	4.86	69
Vocabulary	5	2.49	50
Spelling	20	10.42	52
Total	**45**	**25.93**	**58**

Facility range and number of questions

Facility range	Number of questions at this facility
90–100%	0
60–89%	23
20–59%	21
0–19%	1

Answers and mark scheme: *GaPS 5 Autumn*

Section A: Grammar, punctuation and vocabulary

Question	Answer and marking guidance	Strand reference	Facility %
1	Award **one mark** for **both** correct. When Harry (ran) on the grass, his shoes (got) muddy.	G, G1 G1.2 Verbs	39
2	Award **one mark** for **all** correct. | | Noun | Adjective | |---|---|---| | bravery | ✓ | | | deceitful | | ✓ | | proud | | ✓ |	G, G1 G1.3 Adjectives	16
3	Award **one mark** for **all** lines correct. The children → new gel pen was a present from her friend The child's → were painting the background for the school play The children's → classroom displays had been changed	P, G5 G5.8 Apostrophes	80
4	Award **one mark** for: Ending: **–ation**	G, G1 G1.1 Nouns	18
5	Award **one mark** for: The large crowd cheered (loudly) when the race began.	G, G1 G1.6 Adverbs	64
6	Award **one mark** for: Please can you tell me how long the party will last ☑	P, G5 G5.3 Question marks	74
7	Award **one mark** for **both** answers correct. William Shakespeare **is** / (**was**) born in Stratford-upon-Avon in 1564. Later he **will move** / (**moved**) to London.	G, G4 G4.2 Tense consistency	37
8	Award **one mark** for **both** commas correctly placed. The children could choose to play netball**,** cricket**,** hockey or tennis.	P, G5 G5.5 Commas in lists	72

62 Answers and mark scheme: *GaPS 5 Autumn*

Question	Answer and marking guidance	Strand reference	Facility %
9	Award **one mark** for a correct answer. Indicative answers could be: After the birthday party, After lunch, On Saturday afternoon, Luckily, First, **Do not award** the mark if the comma is not inserted.	G, G1 G1.6a Adverbials	42
10	Award **one mark** for: Walk along the path (that) goes around the edge of the lake.	G, G1 G1.5b Relative pronouns	20
11	Award **one mark** for: across ☑	G, G1 G1.7 Prepositions	96
12	Award **one mark** for all **three** words correctly encircled. (Two) older boys played football on (the) pitch in (the) school field.	G, G1 G1.8 Determiners	9
13	Award **one mark** for: a comma ☑	P, G5 G5.6a Commas to clarify meaning	58
14	Award **one mark** for: "Good night and sleep well ↑✓, ↑ said John ↑.	P, G5 G5.7 Inverted commas	34
15	Award **one mark** for: Jo **(**who had been dancing since he was three**)** had been given a main part in the play.	P, G5 G5.9 Punctuation for parenthesis	56
16	Award **one mark** for **both** correct. You should try to tidy up your bedroom now so ↑✓ that you can watch the film later. ↑✓	G, G4 G4.1c Modal verbs	29
17	Award **one mark** for all **three** words correctly encircled. (She) bought a new dress for (herself) and a blue jumper for (her) Dad. Accept answers that have identified 'her' as a determiner rather than as a pronoun.	G, G1 G1.5 Pronouns	28

Answers and mark scheme: *GaPS 5 Autumn*   63

Question	Answer and marking guidance	Strand reference	Facility %
18	Award **one mark** for: Richard III fought against Henry Tudor <u>who later became Henry VII</u>.	G, G3 G3.1a Relative clauses	33
19	Award **one mark** for: Grandma decided the pasta sauce needed more basil <u>after</u> she had tasted it.	G, G3 G3.4 Subordinating conjunctions and subordinate clauses	38
20	Award **one mark** for all **three** correct. (on)(friday) I read a book about the invasion of the (vikings).	P, G5 G5.1 Capital letters	35
21	Award **one mark** for: Last night we went to see a film. It was great. ☑	P, G5 G5.2 Full stops	47
22	Award **one mark** for a correct answer. Indicative answers could be: <u>Ali walks home</u>. <u>Ali is walking home</u>.	G, G4 G4.2 Tense consistency	38
23	Award **one mark** for: The (fierce) tiger hunted its prey quietly.	G, G1 G1.3 Adjectives	65
24	Award **one mark** for: I was hiding the pencils. ☑	G, G7 G7.1 Standard English	42
25	Award **one mark** for **all** lines correctly drawn. Prefix — Word out — value de — value (de → value) mis — lead inter — act (out → perform, de → value, mis → lead, inter → act)	V, G6 G6.2 Prefixes	50
26	Award **one mark** for **both** correct. I was not aloud / (allowed) to jump on the bed. The hotel welcomed its important (guest) / guessed.	V, G6 G6.5 Homophones and other words that are often confused	76
27	Award **one mark** for a correct answer. Indicative answers could be: <u>auditorium</u> <u>auditory</u>	V, G6 G6.4 Word families	19

Question	Answer and marking guidance	Strand reference	Facility %
28	Award **one mark** for: wasn't	P, G5 G5.8 Apostrophes	61
29	Award **one mark** for: honour ☑	V, G6 G6.1 Synonyms and antonyms	81
30	Award **one mark** for: invented	G, G4 G4.2 Tense consistency	73
31	Award **one mark** for **both** correct. Sarah was (unlucky) to fall over, but (fortunately) her friend was there to help.	V, G6 G6.1 Synonyms and antonyms	72
32	Award **one mark** for **all** correct. | Sentence	Commas used to clarify meaning	Commas used after fronted adverbials
---	---	---
After the birthday party, popped balloons and streamers littered the floor.		✓
Gold watches, for example, are going on sale today.	✓	
As fast as it could, the rabbit ran over the hill.		✓		P, G5 G5.6a Commas to clarify meaning	51
33	Award **one mark** for **both** correct. It was snowing <u>heavily</u> so we built <u>those</u> snowmen. **Also accept**: <u>some</u> snowmen <u>the</u> snowmen	G, G7 G7.1 Standard English	30
34	Award **one** mark for a correctly punctuated sentence that uses a modal verb of certainty, e.g: The class council <u>must / will</u> decide what to do for Golden Time.	G, G4 G4.1c Modal verbs	21
35	Award **one mark** for appropriate re-wording in the past perfect, e.g: The teacher had told the class to work quietly.	G, G4 G4.1b Verbs in the perfect form	23

Section B: Spelling

Question	Answer and marking guidance	Strand reference	Facility %
1	Award **one mark** for: If we **oversleep** we will miss our flight. The correct spelling of the word **oversleep**.	S41 Prefixes (Year 4)	90
2	Award **one mark** for: The ship had problems on the **rough** sea. The correct spelling of the word **rough**.	S59 Words containing the letter string *ough*	63
3	Award **one mark** for: Raj did some **excellent** work on the Tudors. The correct spelling of the word **excellent**.	S55 Words ending in –ant, –ance, –ancy, –ent, –ence, –ency	30
4	Award **one mark** for: The theatre visit was an event of great **importance**. The correct spelling of the word **importance**.	S55 Words ending in –ant, –ance, –ancy, –ent, –ence, –ency	52
5	Award **one mark** for: The man had to prove his **innocence**. The correct spelling of the word **innocence**.	S55 Words ending in –ant, –ance, –ancy, –ent, –ence, –ency	17
6	Award **one mark** for: Our task was to **classify** insects. The correct spelling of the word **classify**.	S37 Common exception words	49
7	Award **one mark** for: The politician did not mean to **mislead** the audience. The correct spelling of the word **mislead**.	S41 Prefixes	59
8	Award **one mark** for: Our plan was to **restructure** the class assembly. The correct spelling of the word **restructure**.	S41 Prefixes	41
9	Award **one mark** for: The snowman **disappeared** after the first sunny day. The correct spelling of the word **disappeared**.	S41 Prefixes	24
10	Award **one mark** for: I had to **deactivate** the alien's laser gun. The correct spelling of the word **deactivate**.	S41 Prefixes	49

Question	Answer and marking guidance	Strand reference	Facility %
11	Award **one mark** for: The **musician** was excellent. The correct spelling of the word **musician**.	S47 Endings that sound like /ʃən/, spelled –tion, –sion, –ssion, –cian	34
12	Award **one mark** for: The **invention** was a big success. The correct spelling of the word **invention**.	S47 Endings that sound like /ʃən/, spelled –tion, –sion, –ssion, –cian	67
13	Award **one mark** for: We learnt about long **division** in maths. The correct spelling of the word **division**.	S45 Endings that sound like /ʒən/	64
14	Award **one mark** for: I had to **measure** five objects in class. The correct spelling of the word **measure**.	S44 Words with endings sounding like /ʒə/ or /tʃə/	57
15	Award **one mark** for: The poem used a lot of **humorous** language. The correct spelling of the word **humorous**.	S46 the suffix –ous	18
16	Award **one mark** for: You need to **justify** your reasons. The correct spelling of the word **justify**.	S37 Common exception words	60
17	Award **one mark** for: I would like to **revisit** Glasgow one day. The correct spelling of the word **revisit**.	S41 Prefixes	66
18	Award **one mark** for: We had to **characterise** King Henry VIII. The correct spelling of the word **characterise**. **Do not** accept characterize.	S48 Words with the /k/ sound spelled ch	30
19	Award **one mark** for: The referee decided to **disallow** the goal. The correct spelling of the word **disallow**.	S41 Prefixes	49
20	Award **one mark** for: The shopping centre **development** was going slowly. The correct spelling of the word **development**.	S37 Common exception words	42

Answers and mark scheme: *GaPS 5 Autumn*

GaPS 5 Autumn: Analysis of performance by strand

Strand	Number of marks available	National average mark	National average %
Grammar	20	6.01	30
Punctuation	10	5.43	54
Vocabulary	5	2.70	54
Spelling	20	9.46	47
Total	**55**	**23.60**	**43**

Facility range and number of questions

Facility range	Number of questions at this facility
90–100%	2
60–89%	15
20–59%	32
0–19%	6

Answers and mark scheme: *GaPS 5 Autumn*

Answers and mark scheme: GaPS 5 Spring

Section A: Grammar, punctuation and vocabulary

Question	Answer and marking guidance	Strand reference	Facility %
1	Award **one** mark for: pretty ☑	V, G6 G6.1 Synonyms and antonyms	94
2	Award **one** mark for **both** correct. My sister Lucy was very silly. <u>She</u> got jam all over <u>her</u> duvet cover. **Accept** <u>she</u>.	G, G1 G1.5 Pronouns	92
3	Award **one** mark for **both** commas correctly placed. Owls, badgers, hedgehogs and bats are all nocturnal animals.	P, G5 G5.5 Commas in lists	87
4	Award **one** mark for: over ☑	G, G1 G1.7 Prepositions	98
5	Award **one** mark for **all** correct. 	Noun	Common	Proper	Abstract
idea			✓
Thursday		✓	
freedom			✓
girl	✓				G, G1 G1.1 Nouns	37
6	Award **one** mark for **all** correct. The film is based on real events. ↑ ↑ ↑ [determiner] [verb] [adjective] **Accept** plausible misspellings.	G, G1 G1 Grammatical terms/word classes	4
7	Award **one** mark for **both** correct. immense ☑ tiny ☑	G, G1 G1.6a Adverbials	54
8	Award **one** mark for **both** correct. The driver couldn't see (clearly) because it was raining (hard).	G, G1 G1.6a Adverbials	28

Question	Answer and marking guidance	Strand reference	Facility %
9	Award **one mark** for: When the waiter came over, I asked which the best ice-creams were. ☑	G, G1 G1.6a Adverbials	36
10	Award **one mark** for **both** correct. William Shakespeare had written / ⟨wrote⟩ plays over four hundred years ago, but they perform / ⟨are performed⟩ today in theatres.	G, G4 G4.2 Tense consistency	23
11	Award **one mark** for: We discussed our holiday to Portugal, ⟨which⟩ Dad is organising.	G, G1 G1.5b Relative pronouns	39
12	Award **one mark** for **three** words correctly encircled. ⟨These⟩ grapes came out of ⟨that⟩ box. They are much tastier than ⟨those⟩ berries.	G, G1 G1.8 Determiners	47
13	Award **one mark** for **both** commas correctly placed. The classroom is, I believe, being decorated in the holiday.	P, G5 G5.6a Commas to clarify meaning	28
14	Award **one mark** for: It had been snowing. ☑	G, G4 G4.1b Verbs in the perfect form	15
15	Award **one mark** for **both** inverted commas correctly placed. The man shouted, "get out of the way!" **Accept** single or double inverted commas. **Also accept** The man shouted, "Get out of the way!"	P, G5 G5.7 Inverted commas	35
16	Award **one mark** for: There is no way – absolutely no way – that I will go on the rollercoaster.	P, G5 G5.9 Punctuation for parenthesis	45
17	Award **one mark** for: Sami will go to the museum tomorrow. ☑	G, G4 G4.1c Modal verbs	64
18	Award **one mark** for: Joe offered an apology, which Freya did not accept.	G, G3 G3.1a Relative clauses	51
19	Award **one mark** for: The children must put their coats on when it is cold.	G, G3 G3.4 Subordinating conjunctions and subordinate clauses	65
20	Award **one mark** for **both** correct. ⟨If⟩ Alex had not checked the weather forecast, she would have been caught in the rain ⟨when⟩ she went into town.	G, G1 G1.4 Conjunctions	43

Answers and mark scheme: *GaPS 5 Spring*

Question	Answer and marking guidance	Strand reference	Facility %
21	Award **one mark** for: Lions live in prides. ☑	G, G2 G2.1 Statements	44
22	Award **one mark** for all **three** correct. |	Formal	Informal
---	---	---
I am writing to complain	✓	
It is my opinion that	✓	
What's more		✓		G, G7 G7.1 Standard English	11
23	Award **one mark** for: were	G, G4 G4.2 Tense consistency	46
24	Award **one mark** for: It's a very good picture. ☑	G, G7 G7.1 Standard English	36
25	Award **one mark** for: To see funny pictures of kittens, (click) here.	G, G2 G2.3 Commands	61
26	Award **one mark** for **all** lines correct. Prefix: re, un, dis, be Word: friend, connect, fasten, visit (re–visit, un–fasten, dis–connect, be–friend)	V, G6 G6.2 Prefixes	48
27	Award **one mark** for **all** correct. 	Noun	ify	ate	ise	en
---	---	---	---	---
dark				✓
assassin		✓		
computer			✓	
simple	✓					G, G1 G1.2 Verbs	52
28	Award **one mark** for **both** correct. The tall building was supported by (steel) / steal girders. I like to have (cereal) / serial for breakfast.	V, G6 G6.5 Homophones and other words that are often confused	69

Question	Answer and marking guidance	Strand reference	Facility %
29	Award **one mark** for a correct answer. Indicative answers could be: hydrogen hydroplane hydrocarbon hydropowered **Do not accept**: hydrate/dehydrate	V, G6 G6.4 Word families	57
30	Award **one mark** for: that ☑	G, G1 G1.5b Relative pronouns	73
31	Award **one mark** for: show ☑	V, G6 G6.4 Word families	11
32	Award **one mark** for: The children's shoes were caked in thick mud.	P, G5 G5.8 Apostrophes	65
33	Award **one mark** for **both** correct. Robert was very (smart;) he had come second in the test of (intelligence).	V, G6 G6.1 Synonyms and antonyms	85
34	Award **one mark** for **both** commas correctly placed. The blue whale, the largest animal to live on Earth, can be up to 30 metres long.	P, G5 G5.6a Commas to clarify meaning	43
35	Award **one mark** for **both** commas correctly placed. John had a piece of string, two marbles, some leaves and a rubber in his pocket.	P, G5 G5.5 Commas in lists	71

Section B: Spelling

Question	Answer and marking guidance	Strand reference	Facility %
1	Award **one mark** for: I was able to **disarm** the alarm by typing in the right code. The correct spelling of the word **disarm**.	S41 Prefixes	54
2	Award **one mark** for: My mum told me to **declutter** my room. The correct spelling of the word **declutter**.	S41 Prefixes	80
3	Award **one mark** for: The school **entrance** was closed. The correct spelling of the word **entrance**.	S55 Words ending in *–ant, –ance, –ancy, –ent, –ence, –ency*	60
4	Award **one mark** for: The homework we were given was **tough** to complete. The correct spelling of the word **tough**.	S59 Words containing the letter string *ough*	47

Question	Answer and marking guidance	Strand reference	Facility %
5	Award **one mark** for: I was **confident** I would win the prize. The correct spelling of the word **confident**.	S55 Words ending in –ant, –ance, –ancy, –ent, –ence, –ency	46
6	Award **one mark** for: We had to **disconnect** the electricity. The correct spelling of the word **disconnect**.	S41 Prefixes	64
7	Award **one mark** for: Amy was always **reliably** on time for art club. The correct spelling of the word **reliably**.	S56 Words ending in –able, –ible, –ably, –ibly	58
8	Award **one mark** for: The new scooter model was **available** at the local shop. The correct spelling of the word **available**.	S56 Words ending in –able, –ible, –ably, –ibly	69
9	Award **one mark** for: Ali was dressed **sensibly** for the weather. The correct spelling of the word **sensibly**.	S56 Words ending in –able, –ible, –ably, –ibly	34
10	Award **one mark** for: The **knight** was very brave. The correct spelling of the word **knight**.	S60 Words with 'silent' letters (i.e. letters whose presence cannot be predicted from the pronunciation of the word)	68
11	Award **one mark** for: My little sister had a high **temperature**. The correct spelling of the word **temperature**.	S37 Common exception words	46
12	Award **one mark** for: I had a **stomach** ache all afternoon. The correct spelling of the word **stomach**.	S37 Common exception words	56
13	Award **one mark** for: I was late **according** to the classroom clock. The correct spelling of the word **according**.	S37 Common exception words	47
14	Award **one mark** for: I was **desperate** to win the race. The correct spelling of the word **desperate**.	S37 Common exception words	36
15	Award **one mark** for: She watched the play with an **observant** eye. The correct spelling of the word **observant**.	S55 Words ending in –ant, –ance, –ancy, –ent, –ence, –ency	50

Answers and mark scheme: *GaPS 5 Spring*

Question	Answer and marking guidance	Strand reference	Facility %
16	Award **one mark** for: My dad can <u>whistle</u> very well. The correct spelling of the word **whistle**.	S60 Words with 'silent' letters (i.e. letters whose presence cannot be predicted from the pronunciation of the word)	77
17	Award **one mark** for: I did not mean to <u>misinform</u> my friend. The correct spelling of the word **misinform**.	S41 Prefixes	30
18	Award **one mark** for: Josh is a <u>dependable</u> classmate. The correct spelling of the word **dependable**.	S56 Words ending in –able, –ible, –ably, –ibly	28
19	Award **one mark** for: The publisher <u>specialises</u> in children's books. The correct spelling of the word **specialises**. **Do not accept:** specializes.	S38 Adding suffixes beginning with vowel letters to words of more than one syllable	27
20	Award **one mark** for: The young man had a scruffy <u>appearance</u>. The correct spelling of the word **appearance**.	S55 Words ending in –ant, –ance, –ancy, –ent, –ence, –ency	59

GaPS 5 Spring: Analysis of performance by strand

Strand	Number of marks available	National average mark	National average %
Grammar	22	10.25	47
Punctuation	7	3.87	55
Vocabulary	6	3.89	65
Spelling	20	10.30	52
Total	55	28.32	51

Facility range and number of questions

Facility range	Number of questions at this facility
90–100%	3
60–89%	15
20–59%	33
0–19%	4

Answers and mark scheme: GaPS 5 Summer

Section A: Grammar, punctuation and vocabulary

Question	Answer and marking guidance	Strand reference	Facility %
1	Award **one mark** for: (Fatima) hopped along the (bench.)	G, G1 G1.1 Nouns	57
2	Award **one mark** for question mark clearly placed before the inverted commas. "I'm going to Disha's to collect a CD. Is that ok**?**" she replied.	P, G5 G5.3 Question marks	50
3	Award **one mark** for: My uncle, (who) is 41, has two children.	G, G1 G1.5b Relative pronouns	47
4	Award **one mark** for: This is my home town. ☑	G, G1 G1.3 Adjectives	58
5	Award **one mark** for a correct answer. Indicative answers could be: *definitely, probably, certainly, surely, possibly, obviously*	G, G1 G1.6 Adverbs	49
6	Award **one mark** for both correct. When I have tidied my bedroom, can I play in the garden? ☑ Can I play in the garden when I have tidied my bedroom? ☑	P, G5 G5 Punctuation	56
7	Award **one mark** for a correctly completed table. <table><tr><th>Noun</th><th>Countable</th><th>Not countable</th></tr><tr><td>book</td><td>✓</td><td></td></tr><tr><td>knowledge</td><td></td><td>✓</td></tr><tr><td>sheep</td><td>✓</td><td></td></tr><tr><td>imagination</td><td></td><td>✓</td></tr></table>	G, G1 G1.1 Nouns	78
8	Award **one mark** for: Ania <u>had</u> played outside for an hour before dinner.	G, G4 G4.1b Verbs in the perfect form	49
9	Award **one mark** for: in the end ☑	V, G6 G6.1 Synonyms and antonyms	77

Question	Answer and marking guidance	Strand reference	Facility %
10	Award **one mark** for all **three** commas correctly placed. At the back of the cupboard, Sarah found some glitter, several pipe cleaners, a tube of blue paint and a small brush.	P, G5 G5.5 Commas in lists	70
11	Award **one mark** for a correctly completed table. |	Correct	Incorrect
---	---	---
I play hockey three times one week.		✓
The library books are one week late.	✓	
You get paid £5 one hour delivering leaflets.		✓		G, G1 G1.8 Determiners	49
12	Award **one mark** for: When the lightning struck James, Harvey fainted. **OR** When the lightning struck, James Harvey fainted.	P, G5 G5.6a Commas to clarify meaning	90
13	Award **one mark** for a correctly completed table. | Sentence	Between	Among
---	---	---
She held the pencil _____ her thumb and fingers.	✓	
The prize was divided _____ John and Sarah.	✓	
He found his lost sock _____ the clothes in the wardrobe.		✓		G, G1 G1.7 Prepositions	39
14	Award **one mark** for both correct. I am terrified – and I mean really scared – to go on the rollercoaster.	P, G5 G5.9 Punctuation for parenthesis	53

Question	Answer and marking guidance	Strand reference	Facility %
15	Award **one mark** for a correctly completed table. | Sentence	Certainty	Possibility
---	---	---
We could go to Greece on holiday.		✓
It will snow tomorrow.	✓	
I won't finish my book tonight.		✓		G, G4 G4.1c Modal verbs	64
16	Award **one mark** for the addition of a suitable relative clause that is punctuated correctly. Indicative answers could be: • *The ice-cream van <u>that stopped outside my house</u> sold many types of ice-cream.* • *The ice-cream van<u>, which was red,</u> sold many types of ice-cream.*	G, G3 G3.1a Relative clauses	41
17	Award **one mark** for both correctly encircled. The <u>heard</u> / (**herd**) of sheep ran away when it saw the wolf. I had a really fancy <u>desert</u> / (**dessert**) at the restaurant.	V, G6 G6.5 Homophones and other words that are often confused	58
18	Award **one mark** for: Firstly ☑	G, G1 G1.4 Conjunctions	67
19	Award **one mark** for a correctly completed table. | Sentence	Can have an exclamation mark	Cannot have an exclamation mark
---	---	---
What a joyful puppy you have	✓	
What are you going to do today		✓
Do not talk to me when I'm working	✓			P, G5 G5.4 Exclamation marks	54
20	Award **one mark** for a correctly completed table. 		Article	Demonstrative	Possessive	Quantifier
---	---	---	---	---
an apple	✓			
my bicycle			✓	
five boys				✓
those people		✓				G, G1 G1.8 Determiners	41

Question	Answer and marking guidance	Strand reference	Facility %
21	Award **one mark** for the addition of a suitable subordinate clause that is punctuated correctly. Indicative answers could be: *Joe went to the local shop <u>to buy some sweets.</u>*	G, G3 G3.4 Subordinating conjunctions and subordinate clauses	55
22	Award **one mark** for all **four** lines correct. Sentence → Type Have you been swimming → question What a star I've been → exclamation Put your knee pads on → command The boy was running → statement	G, G2 G2 Functions of sentences	64
23	Award **one mark** for a correctly completed table. | Sentence	Needs an apostrophe	Does not need an apostrophe
---	---	---
The cat pounced on <u>its</u> toy.		✓
<u>Its</u> just not fair.	✓	
I am so glad <u>its</u> sunny.	✓	
The hotel made <u>its</u> guests feel welcome.		✓		P, G5 G5.8 Apostrophes	48
24	Award **one mark** for all **four** correct. (after) tea I went to the park. (my) friend (peter) was there( )	P, G5 G5.1 Capital letters, G5.2 Full stops	29
25	Award **one mark** for both correct. <u>(My) big brother</u> wants to be <u>a primary school teacher</u> when he is older. **Accept** with or without the determiner.	G, G3 G3.2 Noun phrases	31
26	Award **one mark** for a correct answer. Indicative answers could be: *What a lovely surprise that was!* Exclamation mark must be included for the mark to be awarded.	G, G2 G2.4 Exclamations	27
27	Award **one mark** for all **four** inverted commas and **two** commas correctly placed. "Is it possible," asked Lina, "that I could go skating with my friends?" **Accept** single or double inverted commas.	P, G5 G5.7 Inverted commas	31

Question	Answer and marking guidance	Strand reference	Facility %
28	Award **one mark** for both correct. There was a strong (draught) / draft from the window. I would like to know (whose)/who's gloves these are.	V, G6 G6.5 Homophones and other words that are often confused	25
29	Award **one mark** for a correct answer. Indicative answers could be: • *to spread out* • *to stretch out* • *to make longer*	V, G6 G6.4 Word families	53
30	Award **one mark** for: arrive	G, G4 G4.2 Tense consistency	56
31	Award **one mark** for: daring ☑	V, G6 G6.1 Synonyms and antonyms	31
32	Award **one mark** for a correctly completed table. | Sentence	Possessive pronoun	Relative pronoun
---	---	---
That purple bicycle helmet is <u>mine</u>.	✓	
I wear it when I go on my bike, <u>which</u> my dad bought me.		✓
My bike goes much faster than <u>yours</u>.	✓			G, G1 G1.5a Possessive pronouns, G1.5b Relative pronouns	62
33	Award **one mark** for a correct modal verb of possibility, e.g.: The class council <u>may / might / could</u> decide what to do for Golden Time.	G, G4 G4.1c Modal verbs	40
34	Award **one mark** for both correct. Last Tuesday we <u>were</u> hoping for wet play but it <u>didn't / did not</u> happen.	G, G7 G7.1 Standard English	65
35	Award **one mark** for a response that refers to the comma separating the names in the list of cats, or a response that describes the difference in meaning between the two sentences. Indicative answers: • *In the first one there are only two cats but in the second one there are three.* • *The first sentence shows a cat called Snowy White, but in the second sentence this is actually two cats.*	P, G5 G5.6a Commas to clarify meaning	43

Section B: Spelling

Question	Answer and marking guidance	Strand reference	Facility %
1	Award **one mark** for: I need to **develop** my throwing technique. The correct spelling of the word **develop**.	S37 Common exception words	70
2	Award **one mark** for: We had to **rebuild** our model bridge. The correct spelling of the word **rebuild**.	S41 Prefixes	81
3	Award **one mark** for: She was **deceived** by the book's cover. The correct spelling of the word **deceived**.	S58 Words with the /i:/ sound spelled *ei* after *c*	18
4	Award **one mark** for: Our local **community** group planted lots of trees. The correct spelling of the word **community**.	S37 Common exception words	62
5	Award **one mark** for: The year 6 children were able to **supervise** at playtime. The correct spelling of the word **supervise**. **Do not accept** supervize.	S41 Prefixes	79
6	Award **one mark** for: Rob was given **antibiotics** by the doctor. The correct spelling of the word **antibiotics**.	S41 Prefixes	57
7	Award **one mark** for: I **doubt** he will finish his work. The correct spelling of the word **doubt**.	S60 Words with 'silent' letters (i.e. letters whose presence cannot be predicted from the pronunciation of the word)	58
8	Award **one mark** for: The teacher had to **simplify** his explanation. The correct spelling of the word **simplify**.	S38 Adding suffixes beginning with vowel letters to words of more than one syllable	58
9	Award **one mark** for: The gardener **misidentified** the flowers. The correct spelling of the word **misidentified**.	S41 Prefixes	43
10	Award **one mark** for: The students were told to **discontinue** the newspaper. The correct spelling of the word **discontinue**.	S41 Prefixes	68
11	Award **one mark** for: We had no **definite** plans for the weekend. The correct spelling of the word **definite**.	S37 Common exception words	27
12	Award **one mark** for: My enjoyment of the music was **immediate**. The correct spelling of the word **immediate**.	S37 Common exception words	26

Question	Answer and marking guidance	Strand reference	Facility %
13	Award **one mark** for: I was <u>weary</u> after doing PE all afternoon. The correct spelling of the word **weary**.	S61 Homophones and other words that are often confused	55
14	Award **one mark** for: The painter's <u>signature</u> was clear to see. The correct spelling of the word **signature**.	S37 Common exception words	43
15	Award **one mark** for: My sister uses lots of <u>symbols</u> in her texts. The correct spelling of the word **symbols**.	S37 Common exception words	61
16	Award **one mark** for: I had a big <u>bruise</u> on my knee. The correct spelling of the word **bruise**.	S37 Common exception words	54
17	Award **one mark** for: My keys are <u>attached</u> to a key ring. The correct spelling of the word **attached**.	S37 Common exception words	67
18	Award **one mark** for: Mrs Smith quickly <u>perceived</u> the truth. The correct spelling of the word **perceived**.	S58 The words with the /i:/ sound spelled *ei* after *c*	11
19	Award **one mark** for: I was <u>curious</u> to see what was in the box. The correct spelling of the word **curious**.	S37 Common exception words	63
20	Award **one mark** for: I was <u>twelfth</u> in the queue. The correct spelling of the word **twelfth**.	S37 Common exception words	27

GaPS 5 Summer: Analysis of performance by strand

Strand	Number of marks available	National average mark	National average %
Grammar	20	10.16	51
Punctuation	10	5.14	51
Vocabulary	5	2.38	48
Spelling	20	10.23	51
Total	55	27.91	51

Facility range and number of questions

Facility range	Number of questions at this facility
90–100%	1
60–89%	16
20–59%	36
0–19%	2

Answers and mark scheme: GaPS 6 Autumn

Section A: Grammar, punctuation and vocabulary

Question	Answer and marking guidance	Strand reference	Facility %
1	Award **one** mark for: a noun phrase ☑	G, G3 G3.2 Noun phrases	57
2	Award **one** mark for all **four** words encircled. (One) day, (the) children found (some) treasure in (an) old box.	G, G1 G1.8 Determiners	24
3	Award **one** mark for: In July 1969 the first men landed on the Moon. (tick under second space)	P, G5 G5.6a Commas to clarify meaning	80
4	Award **one** mark for a correctly completed table. | Sentence	Main clause	Subordinate clause
---	---	---
Josh, who had a new bike, went for a ride.		✓
Josh's friend Fahad went too, although it was raining.		✓
They were both soaked when they got home.	✓			G, G3 G3.4 Subordinating conjunctions and subordinate clauses	51
5	Award **one** mark for: Maria opened the new book (that) her aunt had given her.	G, G1 G1.5b Relative pronouns	21
6	Award **one** mark for: Who will win the football trophy this year ☑	G, G2 G2.2 Questions	88
7	Award **one** mark for **both** words encircled. We was / (were) standing in a line. Suzi (was) / were asked to read a poem.	G, G7 G7.1 Standard English	90

Question	Answer and marking guidance	Strand reference	Facility %
8	Award **one mark** for: The blue whale ⇧ is the largest animal ⇧ in the world ⇧✓ when it is fully grown ⇧ it weighs more than 150 tonnes.	P, G5 G5.11 Semi-colons	52
9	Award **one mark** for: are were ☑ or were were ☑	G, G4 G4.2 Tense consistency	87
10	Award **one mark** for: Tidy the chairs before you leave. ☑	G, G2 G2.3 Commands	40
11	Award **one mark** for a correctly completed table. 	Sentence	Modal verb indicates certainty	Modal verb indicates possibility	 |---|---|---| | Mum said we might go to the cinema today. | | ✓ | | You could ask your teacher for help. | | ✓ | | It may be better weather tomorrow. | | ✓ | | I must remember my homework. | ✓ | |	G, G4 G4.1c Modal verbs	55
12	Award **one mark** for all **three** words encircled. (Soon) it became (quite) dark and all the animals scurried (quickly) into the woods.	G, G1 G1.6 Adverbs	14
13	Award **one mark** for **both** words encircled. My dad lost his driving (licence) / license. I advice / (advise) you to take more care.	V, G6 G6.5 Homophones and other words that are often confused	54

Question	Answer and marking guidance	Strand reference	Facility %
14	Award **one mark** for an exclamation, e.g: What a delicious pizza that was/is! How delicious this pizza is! **Accept** minor copying/spelling errors, e.g. What a delicous pizza that was! **Do not accept** answers without: • a verb, e.g. What a delicious pizza! • correct punctuation.	G, G2 G2.4 Exclamations	19
15	Award **one mark** for all **four** words encircled. (florence)(nightingale,) who was a famous nurse, was born in (italy) in (may) 1820.	P, G5 G5.1 Capital letters	63
16	Award **one mark** for: "Do you want to play rounders?" **Accept**: • single inverted commas • minor variations that preserve the basic meaning, e.g. "Would you like to play rounders?" • minor copying/spelling errors, e.g. 'Do you want to play ronders?'	P, G5 G5.7 Inverted commas	41
17	Award **one mark** for all **five** words encircled. The (blazing) sun shone brightly in the (clear)(blue) sky and dazzled the (old) dog as he lay panting in the (dusty) street. **Accept** 'clear' and 'blue' encircled together.	G, G1 G1.3 Adjectives	13
18	Award **one mark** for a correctly completed table. <table><tr><th>Sentence</th><th>Formal</th><th>Informal</th></tr><tr><td>The concert will commence at 7 p.m.</td><td>✓</td><td></td></tr><tr><td>There is loads of rubbish in the playground.</td><td></td><td>✓</td></tr><tr><td>Walking is a fab way to keep fit.</td><td></td><td>✓</td></tr><tr><td>Pupils have benefitted from the new equipment.</td><td>✓</td><td></td></tr></table>	V, G7 G7.2 Formal and informal vocabulary	58

Question	Answer and marking guidance	Strand reference	Facility %
19	Award **one mark** for: won't (with arrow pointing up) **Do not accept** answers: • that are misspelled • without correct punctuation.	P, G5 G5.8 Apostrophes	70
20	Award **one mark** for: <u>water</u> **Accept** answers that are misspelled, e.g. watter.	V, G6 G6.4 Word families	43
21	Award **one mark** for all **three** words encircled. Put the butter and sugar ⟨in⟩ a pan ⟨with⟩ the chocolate and heat gently ⟨on⟩ a stove.	G, G1 G1.7 Prepositions	17
22	Award **one mark** for: <u>fronted adverbial</u> **Accept** answers that are misspelled.	G, G1 G1.6a Adverbials	18
23	Award **one mark** for: Is that the boy ⟨whose⟩ pen you borrowed yesterday?	G, G1 G1.5b Relative pronouns	45
24	Award **one mark** for **both** commas correctly inserted. I had cereal**,** yoghurt**,** toast and orange juice for breakfast.	P, G5 G5.5 Commas in lists	81
25	Award **one mark** for **both** sentences correctly completed. Jake is the boy **whose** bike I borrowed. I want to know **who's** helping in the library today.	V, G6 G6.5 Homophones and other words that are often confused	65
26	Award **one mark** for: <u>dash/dashes</u> **Accept** answers that are misspelled. **Do not accept** hyphen.	P, G5 G5.9 Punctuation for parenthesis	65
27	Award **one mark** for: <u>The pool was freezing cold, wasn't it?</u> **Accept** minor variations/copying errors, e.g. • The pool was frezzing, wasn't it? • The pool was cold, wasn't it? **Do not accept** answers without correct punctuation.	G, G7 G7.3 Formal and informal structures	11

Answers and mark scheme: *GaPS 6 Autumn*

Question	Answer and marking guidance	Strand reference	Facility %
28	Award **one mark** for: They spent the afternoon **lazily** watching television. **Do not accept** answers that are misspelled.	G, G1 G1.6 Adverbs	49
29	Award **one mark** for a grammatically correct sentence containing a relative clause and using correct punctuation, e.g: Adil, who was very tired, went home from school. Adil, whose foot was hurting, went home from school. **Accept** minor copying / spelling errors, e.g. Adil, who was late, went home from scool. **Do not accept** responses that: • use a phrase instead of a subordinate clause, e.g: Adil went home from school, wearing his coat. • add another main clause, e.g: Adil went home from school and had tea. • include punctuation errors, e.g: adil who was hungry went home from school	G, G3 G3.1a Relative clauses	26
30	Award **one mark** for all **three** boxes correctly labelled. Abi liked ice-cream. S V O	G, G1 G1.9 Subject and object	71
31	Award **one mark** for inverted commas correctly inserted: "It's time to come home, Dad," said Kamil. "It's nearly time for tea." **Accept** single or double inverted commas.	P, G5 G5.7 Inverted commas	62
32	Award **one mark** for an explanation of both pupils and pupils', e.g: In the first sentence pupils is in the plural so it doesn't need an apostrophe. In the second sentence, pupils' has an apostrophe because it is the parents of the pupils/the pupils belonging to the parents. **Also accept:** • the second sentence has a possessive apostrophe • answers that are not written as full sentences. **Do not accept** answers that explain only one sentence.	P, G5 G5.8 Apostrophes	17
33	Award **one mark** for: Can you device / (devise) a different way of doing this experiment?	V, G6 G6.5 Homophones and other words that are often confused	80

Question	Answer and marking guidance	Strand reference	Facility %
34	Award **one mark** for: <u>parenthesis</u> **Accept** answers that are misspelled. **Also accept** 'to give additional information'. or 'to tell us more about Miss Hussein'.	P, G5 G5.9 Punctuation for parenthesis	68
35	Award **one mark** for: <u>They</u> **Do not accept** answers without a capital letter.	G, G1 G1.5 Pronouns	57

Section B: Spelling

Question	Answer and marking guidance	Strand reference	Facility %
1	Award **one mark** for: John went through the <u>automatic</u> door of the shop. The correct spelling of the word **automatic**.	S41 Prefixes	77
2	Award **one mark** for: The cheap shoes were a <u>bargain</u>. The correct spelling of the word **bargain**.	S37 Common exception words	59
3	Award **one mark** for: Eva watched her favourite television <u>programme</u>. The correct spelling of the word **programme**.	S37 Common exception words (Year 5)	38
4	Award **one mark** for: The children saw the kitten <u>disappear</u> behind the tree. The correct spelling of the word **disappear**.	S41 Prefixes	45
5	Award **one mark** for: Mrs Khan is very <u>ambitious</u> for her son. The correct spelling of the word **ambitious**.	S53 Endings which sound like/ʃəs/spelled –cious or –tious	53
6	Award **one mark** for: The old lady was behaving in a <u>suspicious</u> way. The correct spelling of the word **suspicious**.	S53 Endings which sound like/ʃəs/spelled –cious or –tious	52
7	Award **one mark** for: The orange juice tasted <u>artificial</u>. The correct spelling of the word **artificial**.	S54 Endings which sound like/ʃəl/spelled –cial, –tial	51
8	Award **one mark** for: Are you going to the <u>leisure</u> centre today? The correct spelling of the word **leisure**.	S37 Common exception words	40
9	Award **one mark** for: Everyone had to <u>queue</u> to get onto the bus. The correct spelling of the word **queue**.	S37 Common exception words	43

Answers and mark scheme: *GaPS 6 Autumn*

Question	Answer and marking guidance	Strand reference	Facility %
10	Award **one mark** for: Mr Jones told us not to **exaggerate**. The correct spelling of the word **exaggerate**.	S37 Common exception words	26
11	Award **one mark** for: I had the **opportunity** to play for England. The correct spelling of the word **opportunity**.	S37 Common exception words	26
12	Award **one mark** for: Finishing the model was an **achievement** for Ali. The correct spelling of the word **achievement**.	S37 Common exception words	36
13	Award **one mark** for: Dina was **determined** to get into the team. The correct spelling of the word **determined**.	S37 Common exception words	48
14	Award **one mark** for: Who would like to visit the Houses of **Parliament**? The correct spelling of the word **Parliament**. **Accept** answers without a capital letter.	S37 Common exception words	21
15	Award **one mark** for: Feeling tired can **affect** your ability to work. The correct spelling of the word **affect**.	S61 Homophones and others words that are often confused	61
16	Award **one mark** for: Read these **environmental** tips for children. The correct spelling of the word **environmental**.	S37 Common exception words	19
17	Award **one mark** for: Cross-country running is **physically** tough. The correct spelling of the word **physically**.	S37 Common exception words	29
18	Award **one mark** for: Try not to **criticise** other children. The correct spelling of the word **criticise**.	S37 Common exception words	19
19	Award **one mark** for: Sun-cream is **essential** on a hot day. The correct spelling of the word **essential**.	S54 Endings which sound like /ʃəl/ spelled –cial, –tial	38
20	Award **one mark** for: I **especially** like chocolate cake. The correct spelling of the word **especially**.	S54 Endings which sound like /ʃəl/ spelled –cial, –tial	40

GaPS 6 Autumn: Analysis of performance by strand

Strand	Number of marks available	National average mark	National average %
Grammar	20	7.99	40
Punctuation	10	5.44	54
Vocabulary	5	2.75	55
Spelling	20	8.09	40
Total	**55**	**24.27**	**44**

Facility range and number of questions

Facility range	Number of questions at this facility
90–100%	1
60–89%	14
20–59%	31
0–19%	9

Answers and mark scheme: GaPS 6 Spring

Section A: Grammar, punctuation and vocabulary

Question	Answer and marking guidance	Strand reference	Facility %
1	Award **one mark** for all **three** words encircled. Mum likes to sing (whilst) cleaning the car. Mr Patel has been sad (since) his cat disappeared. (Unless) you are careful, you will lose your gloves.	G, G3 G3.3 Co-ordinating conjunctions and subordinate clauses	58
2	Award **one mark** for: The small, dusty room looked (dismal) and menacing in the evening light.	V, G6 G6.1 Synonyms and antonyms	73
3	Award **one mark** for a correctly completed table. | Sentence	Noun	Verb
---	---	---
Tomorrow I am going for a <u>run</u>.	✓	
<u>Wheel</u> your bicycle home carefully.		✓
Ali wanted to <u>race</u> his friend to school.		✓		G, G1 G1.1 Nouns, G1.2 Verbs	26
4	Award **one mark** for all **six** words encircled. On (december) 14th, 1911, (roald) (amundsen) and four other (norwegian) explorers were the first people to reach the (south) (pole). **Accept** 'roald' and 'amundsen' and 'south' and 'pole' encircled together in each case.	P, G5 G5.1 Capital letters	65
5	Award **one mark** for **both** words encircled. I (did) / done my music practice this morning. There was / (were) three pigeons in the garden.	G, G7 G7.1 Standard English	77
6	Award **one mark** for: bullet points/bullets **Accept** answers that are misspelled. **Do not accept** 'colon' as it is not in the list.	P, G5 G5.14 Bullet points	78

Question	Answer and marking guidance	Strand reference	Facility %
7	Award **one mark** for all **three** words encircled. (Several) pupils spent (their) breaks helping with (the) school garden.	G, G1 G1.8 Determiners	38
8	Award **one mark** for: The children cannot play outside today. **Accept:** • minor variations in wording which use formal language, e.g. The children/young people are unable to play outside the house today. • spelling errors, e.g. The children canot play outside today. **Do not accept** answers without correct punctuation.	V, G7 G7.2 Formal and informal vocabulary	44
9	Award **one mark** for: I have lost the pen (that) Aamirah lent me yesterday.	G, G1 G1.5b Relative pronouns	47
10	Award **one mark** for **both** commas correctly inserted. My favourite sports are football, basketball, cricket and darts.	P, G5 G5.5 Commas in lists	88
11	Award **one mark** for **both** words encircled. The children go to their local park but (cant) go on the swings because (theyre) broken.	P, G5 G5.8 Apostrophes	76
12	Award **one mark** for: Ahmed was very <u>creative</u> and painted a beautiful picture. **Do not accept** answers that are misspelled.	G, G1 G1.3 Adjectives	73
13	Award **one mark** for: <u>Are the sheep and goats in the field?</u> **Accept** minor copying errors e.g. Are the sheep and goats in the feild? **Do not accept** answers without correct punctuation.	G, G2 G2.2 Questions	68
14	Award **one mark** for **both** words correctly encircled. Mrs Lee is the (principal)/ principle of the senior school. The mountaineers began their (ascent)/ assent of Everest.	V, G6 G6.5 Homophones and other words that are often confused	34

Question	Answer and marking guidance	Strand reference	Facility %
15	Award **one mark** for a correctly completed table. | Sentence	Modal verb indicates certainty	Modal verb indicates possibility
---	---	---
Mum said we might go swimming tomorrow.		✓
You must wash your hands before meals.	✓	
Jess may have a part in the school play.		✓
The lesson will be over in ten minutes.	✓			G, G4 G4.1c Modal verbs	84
16	Award **one mark** for **both** ticks correct. Jan the tallest boy in the class is very ✓ ✓ good at basketball.	P, G5 G5.9 Punctuation for parenthesis	79
17	Award **one mark** for: The house which was once magnificent ✓ is now just an old ruin in the middle of nowhere.	G, G3 G3.1a Relative clauses	83
18	Award **one mark** for: semi-colon **Accept** answers that are misspelled.	P, G5 G5.11 Semi-colons	53
19	Award **one mark** for: "Yes," said John. "You can help me choose a new phone." ☑	P, G5 G5.7 Inverted commas	63
20	Award **one mark** for a correct sentence using the word lift as a noun, e.g. • We took the **lift** to the second floor. • My mum gave my friend a **lift** in her car. **Accept** answers with misspellings. **Do not accept** answers without correct punctuation.	G, G1 G1.1 Nouns	64

Question	Answer and marking guidance	Strand reference	Facility %
21	Award **one mark** for a correctly completed table. | Sentence	Subject	Object
---	---	---
<u>Leda</u> threw the ball.	✓	
<u>Ms Jones</u> drank tea.	✓	
Zak opened the <u>box</u>.		✓
The pupils waved <u>flags</u>.		✓		G, G1 G1.9 Subject and object	86
22	Award **one mark** for all **four** words correctly matched. il — legal im — possible dis — advantage mis — taken	V, G6 G6.2 Prefixes	92
23	Award **one mark** for the sentence rewritten with a subordinate clause and correct punctuation, e.g. • After he'd eaten his dinner, the dog ran away. • The dog ran away when he saw the man. • The dog, which was growling fiercely, ran away. **Accept** answers with misspellings. **Do not accept** answers without correct punctuation.	G, G3 G3.4 Subordinating conjunctions and subordinate clauses	50
24	Award **one mark** for a possessive pronoun, e.g. • mine • ours • theirs • his/hers **Do not accept** misspellings.	G, G1 G1.5a Possessive pronouns	67
25	Award **one mark** for **both** answers correct. Sixty-five pupils from Thurby Primary School took [hyphen points to the hyphen in Sixty-five] part in the race – to raise money for charity. [dash points to the dash] **Accept** answers that are misspelled.	P, G5 G5.13 Hyphens, G5.12 Single dashes	61

Question	Answer and marking guidance	Strand reference	Facility %
26	Award **one mark** for: Moreover ☑	G, G1 G1.6a Adverbials	53
27	Award **one mark** for: On Saturday three buses broke down in the centre of town**;** this caused a terrible traffic jam so the police were called.	P, G5 G5.11 Semi-colons	68
28	Award **one mark** for **both** words encircled. Zara was (furious) when she slipped on the muddy grass and let in a goal. The team was delighted when they won the match, but Zara was still (angry) with herself.	V, G6 G6.1 Synonyms and antonyms	78
29	Award **one mark** for **both** words encircled. a question tag ☑	G, G7 G7.3 Formal and informal structures	83
30	Award **one mark** for all **four** pairs correctly matched. daring — miserable humble — arrogant generous — mean joyful — timid (daring–timid and humble–arrogant and generous–mean and joyful–miserable matched appropriately as antonyms)	V, G6 G6.1 Synonyms and antonyms	45
31	Award **one mark** for: There are seven continents in the world**:** Africa Antarctica Asia Australia Europe North America and South America.	P, G5 G5.10 Colons	81
32	Award **one mark** for a sentence with a **fronted adverbial**, correctly punctuated, e.g. • After three days, the circus left town. • Last Monday, the circus left town. • Unexpectedly, the circus left town. **Accept** answers with copying errors/misspellings. **Do not accept** answers without correct punctuation.	G, G1 G1.6a Adverbials	56
33	Award **one mark** for: hyphen ☑	P, G5 G5.13 Hyphens	64

Question	Answer and marking guidance	Strand reference	Facility %
34	Award **one mark** for an explanation of 'you'll', e.g. 'You'll' is short for you will/is a contraction **and** the apostrophe marks where letters/w and i have been left out. **AND** 'Lucy's', e.g. Apostrophe s after Lucy means belonging to Lucy/shows Lucy owns the shoes. **Accept** answers that are not written as full sentences.	P, G5 G5.8 Apostrophes	59
35	Award **one mark** for: (1) 'They' should go here because • it is referring to the flowers • it is followed by/is the subject of 'were', a plural verb (2) 'she' should go here because this refers to 'my mum'/she is the subject of 'loved' **Accept** answers that are not written as full sentences.	G, G1 G1.5 Pronouns	34

Section B: Spelling

Question	Answer and marking guidance	Strand reference	Facility %
1	Award **one mark** for: Meera **misunderstood** what the teacher said. The correct spelling of the word **misunderstood**.	S41 Prefixes	77
2	Award **one mark** for: She was the **luckiest** girl in the world. The correct spelling of the word **luckiest**.	S38 Adding suffixes beginning with vowel letters to words of more than one syllable	74
3	Award **one mark** for: Complete the **application** form to join the team. The correct spelling of the word **application**.	S47 Endings that sound like /ʃən/, spelled –tion, –sion, –ssion, –cian	66
4	Award **one mark** for: The **vehicle** was parked outside. The correct spelling of the word **vehicle**.	S37 Common exception words	38

Question	Answer and marking guidance	Strand reference	Facility %
5	Award **one mark** for: Class 6 visited an **ancient** castle. The correct spelling of the word **ancient**.	S37 Common exception words	48
6	Award **one mark** for: End your letter to Mr Brown with 'Yours **sincerely**'. The correct spelling of the word **sincerely**.	S37 Common exception words	73
7	Award **one mark** for: Next term there will be an art **competition**. The correct spelling of the word **competition**.	S37 Common exception words	36
8	Award **one mark** for: I don't want to **embarrass** my friend. The correct spelling of the word **embarrass**.	S37 Common exception words	52
9	Award **one mark** for: I like poems that **rhyme**. The correct spelling of the word **rhyme**.	S37 Common exception words	43
10	Award **one mark** for: Sam was always getting into **mischief**. The correct spelling of the word **mischief**.	S37 Common exception words	58
11	Award **one mark** for: **Persuade** your friends to help you. The correct spelling of the word **persuade**. **Accept** answers without a capital letter.	S37 Common exception words	37
12	Award **one mark** for: Sign language is a kind of **communication**. The correct spelling of the word **communication**.	S37 Common exception words	67
13	Award **one mark** for: It was a **disastrous** school trip. The correct spelling of the word **disastrous**.	S46 The suffix –*ous*	46
14	Award **one mark** for: A spider hung from the **ceiling**. The correct spelling of the word **ceiling**.	S37 Common exception words	66
15	Award **one mark** for: The school sound **system** was broken. The correct spelling of the word **system**.	S37 Common exception words	63

Question	Answer and marking guidance	Strand reference	Facility %
16	Award **one mark** for: The story was about a brave <u>knight</u> and a dragon. The correct spelling of the word **knight**.	S60 Words with 'silent' letters (i.e. letters whose presence cannot be predicted from the pronunciation of the word)	35
17	Award **one mark** for: <u>Occupy</u> yourself by helping Mr Green. The correct spelling of the word **occupy**. **Accept** answers without a capital letter.	S37 Common exception words	59
18	Award **one mark** for: The children went to the zoo to <u>observe</u> the animals. The correct spelling of the word **observe**.	S37 Common exception words	79
19	Award **one mark** for: Write your <u>explanation</u> in your exercise book. The correct spelling of the word **explanation**.	S47 Endings that sound like /ʃən/, spelled –tion, –sion, –ssion, –cian	90
20	Award **one mark** for: She answered the question quickly, without <u>hesitation</u>. The correct spelling of the word **hesitation**.	S47 Endings that sound like /ʃən/, spelled –tion, –sion, –ssion, –cian	52

GaPS 6 Spring: Analysis of performance by strand

Strand	Number of marks available	National average mark	National average %
Grammar	17	10.17	60
Punctuation	12	8.09	67
Vocabulary	6	3.58	60
Spelling	20	12.17	61
Total	55	34.01	62

Facility range and number of questions

Facility range	Number of questions at this facility
90–100%	2
60–89%	29
20–59%	24
0–19%	0

Answers and mark scheme: GaPS 6 Summer

Section A: Grammar, punctuation and vocabulary

Question	Answer and marking guidance	Strand reference	Facility %
1	Award **one mark** for all **three** correct. The children are visiting **their** cousins' house. **They're** staying **there** for the afternoon.	V, G6 G6.5 Homophones and other words that are often confused	83
2	Award **one mark** for both brackets correctly placed. Glaciers (formed of thick layers of snow and ice) look static but are actually moving very slowly.	P, G5 G5.9 Punctuation for parenthesis	55
3	Award **one mark** for **all three** words circled. We are throwing away (more) rubbish than ever, according to (the) latest report. This is despite (many) people's efforts to recycle.	G, G1 G1.8 Determiners	18
4	Award **one mark** for a correctly punctuated question, e.g.: • *Have you eaten all the vegetables on your plate?* • *Are you eating all the vegetables on your plate?* **Accept** minor variations in wording / spelling errors, e.g.: • *Have you eaten all your vegetables?* • *Will you eat all the vegetables on your plate?* • *Are you eating your vegetables?* **Do not accept** answers without correct punctuation.	G, G2 G2.2 Questions	71
5	Award **one mark** for: ellipsis **Accept** answers that are misspelled.	P, G5 G5 Punctuation	88
6	Award **one mark** for all words correctly matched. minute — tiny complex — elaborate positive — optimistic genuine — valid	V, G6 G6.1 Synonyms and antonyms	42

Question	Answer and marking guidance	Strand reference	Facility %
7	Award **one mark** for: *Exercise at least three times a week.* **Accept** minor variations / spelling errors e.g.: • *Take exercise at least three times a week.* • *Exercise at least three times a week.* **Do not accept** answers without correct punctuation.	G, G2 G2.3 Commands	64
8	Award **one mark** for the sentence correctly written in the past tense, e.g.: • *It got dark and the old man lit a candle and fed his cat.* • *It was getting dark and the old man was lighting a candle and feeding his cat.* **Accept**: • a combination of verbs in the past progressive and simple past, e.g.: *It was getting dark and the old man lit the candle and fed his cat.* • minor copying / spelling errors, e.g.: *It got dark and the old man lit a candel and was feeding his cat.*	G, G4 G4.1a Simple past and simple present, G4.1d Present and past progressive	63
9	Award **one mark** for both correct. Sam wants to go shopping so she can buy a new top but it is late so she might have to wait until another day.	G, G4 G4.1c Modal verbs	71
10	Award **one mark** for: They don't want to visit the castle because they <u>have been</u> there before. **Do not accept** spelling errors.	G, G4 G4.1b Verbs in the perfect form	40
11	Award **one mark** for: a tent and mats ☑	G, G1 G1.5 Pronouns	75
12	Award **one mark** for: The children ran **enthusiastically** round the track. **Do not accept** answers that are misspelled.	G, G1 G1.6 Adverbs	32
13	Award **one mark** for: She put the bridal/ (bridle) on her pony. Mum is going to (alter)/ altar my costume for me.	V, G6 G6.5 Homophones and other words that are often confused	59

Answers and mark scheme: *GaPS 6 Summer* 99

Question	Answer and marking guidance	Strand reference	Facility %
14	Award **one mark** for: Travelling to London was a long, hard journey – the longest I had ever been on.	P, G5 G5.12 Single dashes	75
15	Award **one mark** for the sentence written with an expanded noun phrase, e.g.: • *I fed the hungry goat.* • *I fed the small, grumpy goat.* • *I fed the lazy goat lying in the shed.* **Accept** misspellings. **Do not accept** answers without correct punctuation.	G, G3 G3.2 Noun phrases	63
16	Award **one mark** for: a relative clause ☑	G, G3 G3.1a Relative clauses	76
17	Award **one mark** for: My friend Lou has lots of pets: dogs, cats, hamsters and budgies.	P, G5 G5.10 Colons, G5.5 Commas in lists	69
18	Award **one mark** for: exclamation ☑	G, G2 G2.4 Exclamations	62
19	Award **one mark** for: My mum is going to drive us to school. ☑	G, G1 G1.2 Verbs	59
20	Award **one mark** for: "It's time to go home now," said Gran, "before it gets too late." **Accept** single or double inverted commas.	P, G5 G5.7 Inverted commas, G5.6a Commas to clarify meaning	41
21	Award **one mark** for both correct. We did enjoy ourselves yesterday. ☑ You were the last person to leave. ☑	G, G7 G7.1 Standard English	26
22	Award **one mark** for: The crane lifted the lorry. 　　S　　V　　O	G, G1 G1.9 Subject and object	69
23	Award **one mark** for all **three** apostrophes correctly placed. "**Ben's** lost his shoes," said Dad. "He **can't** find them anywhere. He thinks **he's** left them in the **boys'** changing rooms."	P, G5 G5.8 Apostrophes	29
24	Award **one mark** for: on the other hand ☑	G, G1 G1.6a Adverbials	67

Question	Answer and marking guidance	Strand reference	Facility %
25	Award **one mark** for both inverted commas and the question mark correctly placed. "Can I go to the cinema?" Martha asked her mum. **Accept** single or double inverted commas and minor variations / spelling errors, e.g.: Martha asked, 'Can I go to the cinema?' **Do not accept** answers without correct punctuation.	P, G5 G5.7 Inverted commas	52
26	Award **one mark** for: modern ☑	V, G6 G6.1 Synonyms and antonyms	45
27	Award **one mark** for: The animals are making a lot of noise, aren't they? **Accept** minor copying /spelling errors, e.g.: The animals are making a noise, aren't they? **Do not accept** answers without correct punctuation.	G, G2 G2.2 Questions	48
28	Award **one mark** for: subjunctive ☑	G, G4 G4.3 Subjunctive verb forms	48
29	Award **one mark** for: Last weekend we went to Wales a beautiful part of the country to see our friends who live there. (arrows indicating commas after "Wales" ☑ and after "country" ☑)	P, G5 G5.9 Punctuation for parenthesis	65
30	Award **one mark** for: The little girl was followed by the scruffy dog. **Accept** minor variations / copying errors, e.g.: The little girl was followed by the dog. **Do not accept** answers without correct punctuation.	G, G4 G4.4 Passive and active	60
31	Award **one mark** for: He wished he were able to run fast enough to win the race. ☑	G, G4 G4.3 Subjunctive verb forms	49

Question	Answer and marking guidance	Strand reference	Facility %
32	Award **one mark** for: To make a model volcano, you will need: • a plastic bottle • some newspaper • glue • masking tape. **Accept**: • minor variations / copying errors e.g. 'newspaper' instead of 'some newspaper' • semi-colons at the end of the first three bullet points • answers without a comma after 'volcano'.	P, G5 G5.14 Bullet points	57
33	Award **one mark** for: There is the woman **who** helped me when I fell over. **AND** An explanation that the relative pronoun 'who' was chosen because it refers to a person (and not a thing), e.g.: • (It's 'who') because it is about a woman. • (I chose who) because it is talking about a person. • It would be which / that about a thing. **Accept** answers that are not written in full sentences.	G, G1 G1.5b Relative pronouns	36
34	Award **one mark** for: The man I asked did not know where the school was. **AND** Explanation of **two** of the following, e.g.: • I changed 'bloke' because it is slang / not the proper word for man. • 'didn't' is a contraction / shortened version (of did not). • 'didn't have a clue' is an idiom / colloquial / conversational / non-literal phrase / what you say rather than write. **Accept** answers that are not written in full sentences. **Do not accept** answers which use the term 'informal language', e.g.: • I changed 'didn't' because it's informal.	V, G7 G7.2 Formal and informal vocabulary	29

102 Answers and mark scheme: *GaPS 6 Summer*

Question	Answer and marking guidance	Strand reference	Facility %
35	Award **one mark** for an explanation that the first sentence refers to the naming of the cat, e.g.: • It means you should call your cat by the name Tom. • The cat is called Tom. **AND** An explanation that the second sentence refers to calling the cat, i.e. summoning it / is addressed to the person named Tom, e.g.: • It means the person you're talking to is called Tom. • 'Calling the cat' means shouting for the cat to come. **Accept** answers that are not written in full sentences. **Do not accept** answers which refer to the function of the comma, e.g.: • The comma makes the meaning clear.	P, G5 G5.6a Commas to clarify meaning	46

Section B: Spelling

Question	Answer and marking guidance	Strand reference	Facility %
1	Award **one mark** for: My friend's **father** is a firefighter. The correct spelling of the word **father**.	S61 Homophones and other words that are often confused	84
2	Award **one mark** for: Have you got all your **equipment** for school? The correct spelling of the word **equipment**.	S37 Common exception words	77
3	Award **one mark** for: My dad carries my little sister on his **shoulders**. The correct spelling of the word **shoulders**.	S37 Common exception words	86
4	Award **one mark** for: Do you **recognise** the girl who helped you? The correct spelling of the word **recognise**. **Do not accept** recognize.	S37 Common exception words	72
5	Award **one mark** for: We **rely** on your support for the team. The correct spelling of the word **rely**.	S37 Common exception words	65
6	Award **one mark** for: She was found **innocent** of eating the last cake. The correct spelling of the word **innocent**.	S55 Words ending in –ant, –ance, –ancy, –ent, –ence, –ency	66

Question	Answer and marking guidance	Strand reference	Facility %
7	Award **one mark** for: It's <u>awkward</u> walking with crutches. The correct spelling of the word **awkward**.	S37 Common exception words	69
8	Award **one mark** for: Layla is taller than <u>average</u>. The correct spelling of the word **average**.	S37 Common exception words	77
9	Award **one mark** for: My auntie is a kind, <u>considerate</u> person. The correct spelling of the word **considerate**.	S37 Common exception words	67
10	Award **one mark** for: Ben has hurt a <u>muscle</u> in his leg. The correct spelling of the word **muscle**.	S37 Common exception words	78
11	Award **one mark** for: I <u>appreciate</u> the help my teacher gives me. The correct spelling of the word **appreciate**.	S37 Common exception words	59
12	Award **one mark** for: Mum went next door to see our <u>neighbour</u>. The correct spelling of the word **neighbour**.	S37 Common exception words	69
13	Award **one mark** for: Did you <u>achieve</u> your target in maths? The correct spelling of the word **achieve**.	S37 Common exception words	66
14	Award **one mark** for: My brother has a toy sailing <u>yacht</u>. The correct spelling of the word **yacht**.	S37 Common exception words	59
15	Award **one mark** for: Jo sorted the pencils <u>systematically</u>. The correct spelling of the word **systematically**.	S43 The suffix –*ly*	33
16	Award **one mark** for: There was <u>controversy</u> over the building of the new school. The correct spelling of the word **controversy**.	S37 Common exception words	48
17	Award **one mark** for: Is there <u>sufficient</u> room in the hall for all the children? The correct spelling of the word **sufficient**.	S37 Common exception words	42
18	Award **one mark** for: Irena's new watch has a <u>guarantee</u>. The correct spelling of the word **guarantee**.	S37 Common exception words	35

Question	Answer and marking guidance	Strand reference	Facility %
19	Award **one mark** for: School lunches are very **nutritious**. The correct spelling of the word **nutritious**.	S53 Endings which sound like /ʃəs/ spelled –cious or –tious	27
20	Award **one mark** for: Warm coats are **necessary** in winter. The correct spelling of the word **necessary**.	S37 Common exception words	34

GaPS 6 Summer: Analysis of performance by strand

Strand	Number of marks available	National average mark	National average %
Grammar	20	10.56	53
Punctuation	10	5.50	55
Vocabulary	5	2.51	50
Spelling	20	11.59	58
Total	55	30.16	55

Facility range and number of questions

Facility range	Number of questions at this facility
90–100%	0
60–89%	28
20–59%	26
0–19%	1

gaps Record Sheet
Pupil name ....

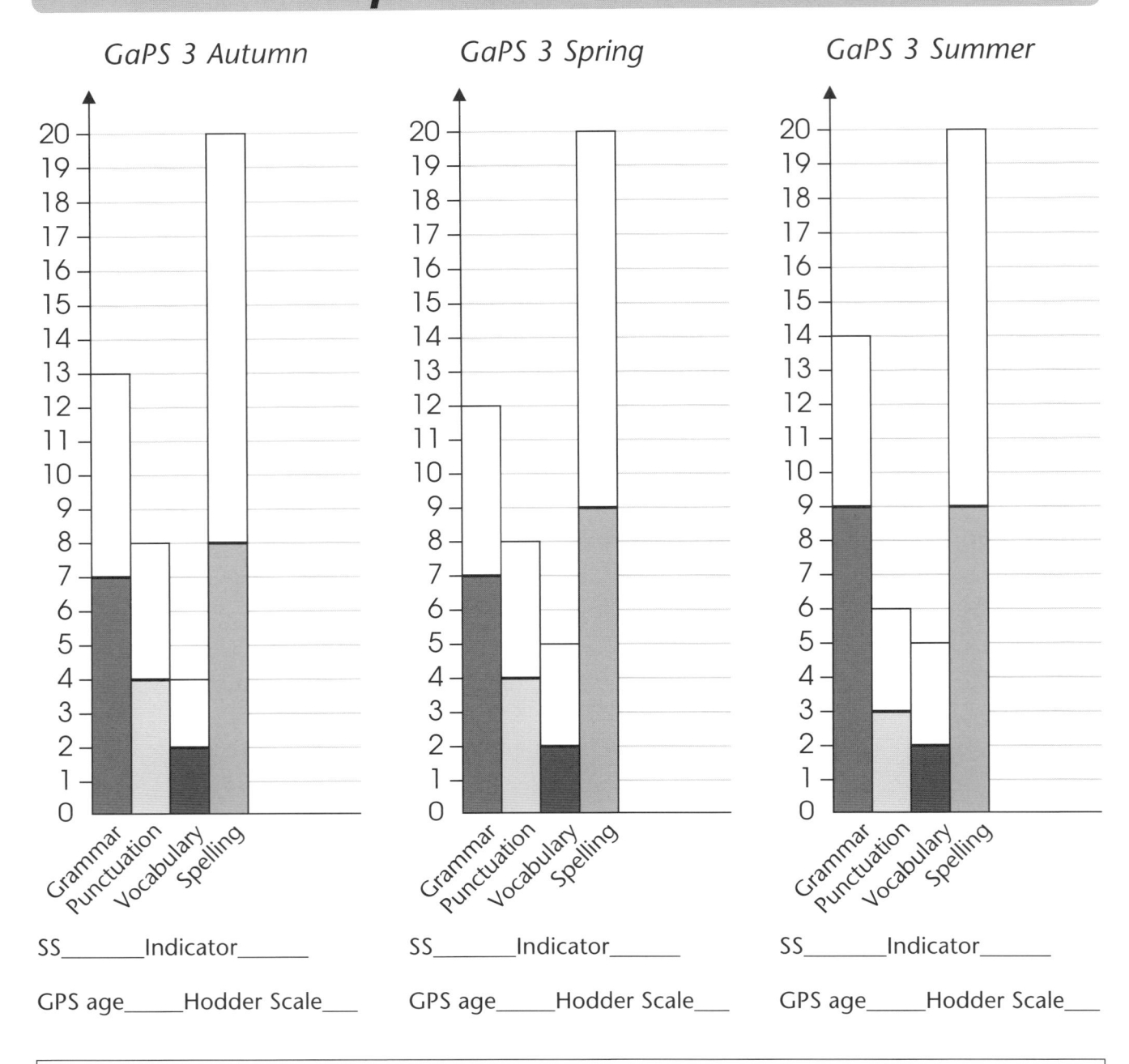

GaPS 3 Autumn

(Bar chart: Grammar 13, Punctuation 8, Vocabulary 4, Spelling 20; national average tints: Grammar 7, Punctuation 4, Vocabulary 2, Spelling 8)

SS_____ Indicator_____

GPS age_____ Hodder Scale___

GaPS 3 Spring

(Bar chart: Grammar 12, Punctuation 8, Vocabulary 5, Spelling 20; national average tints: Grammar 7, Punctuation 4, Vocabulary 2, Spelling 9)

SS_____ Indicator_____

GPS age_____ Hodder Scale___

GaPS 3 Summer

(Bar chart: Grammar 14, Punctuation 6, Vocabulary 5, Spelling 20; national average tints: Grammar 9, Punctuation 3, Vocabulary 2, Spelling 9)

SS_____ Indicator_____

GPS age_____ Hodder Scale___

Note: The tints show the national average scores obtained in the standardisation trial, rounded to whole marks.

© Rising Stars UK Ltd 2018. You may photocopy this page.

106 Record Sheet

gaps Record Sheet
Pupil name ....

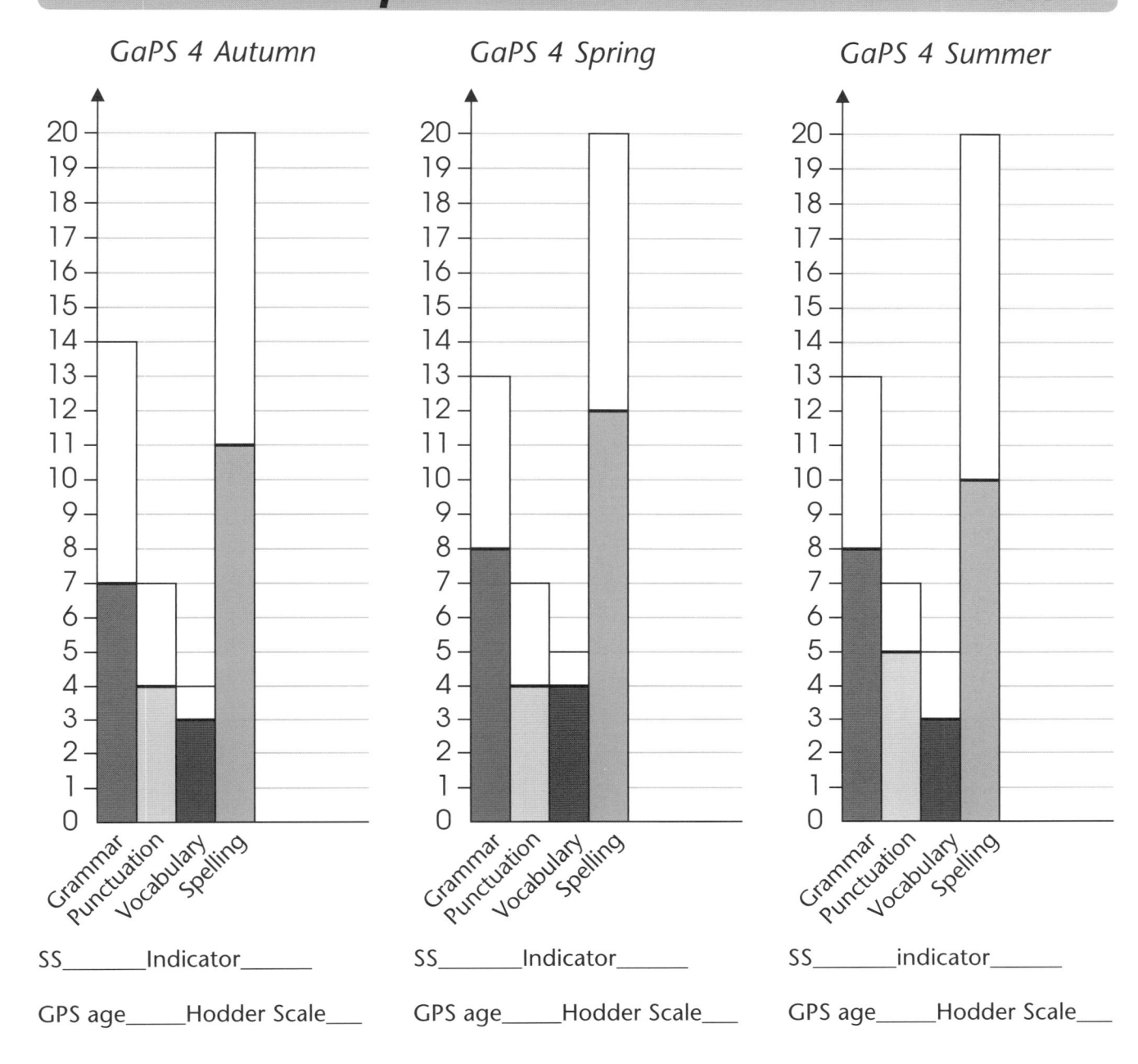

GaPS 4 Autumn

SS_____Indicator_____

GPS age_____Hodder Scale___

GaPS 4 Spring

SS_____Indicator_____

GPS age_____Hodder Scale___

GaPS 4 Summer

SS_____indicator_____

GPS age_____Hodder Scale___

Note: The tints show the national average scores obtained in the standardisation trial, rounded to whole marks.

© Rising Stars UK Ltd 2018. You may photocopy this page.

Record Sheet

gaps Record Sheet
Pupil name ....

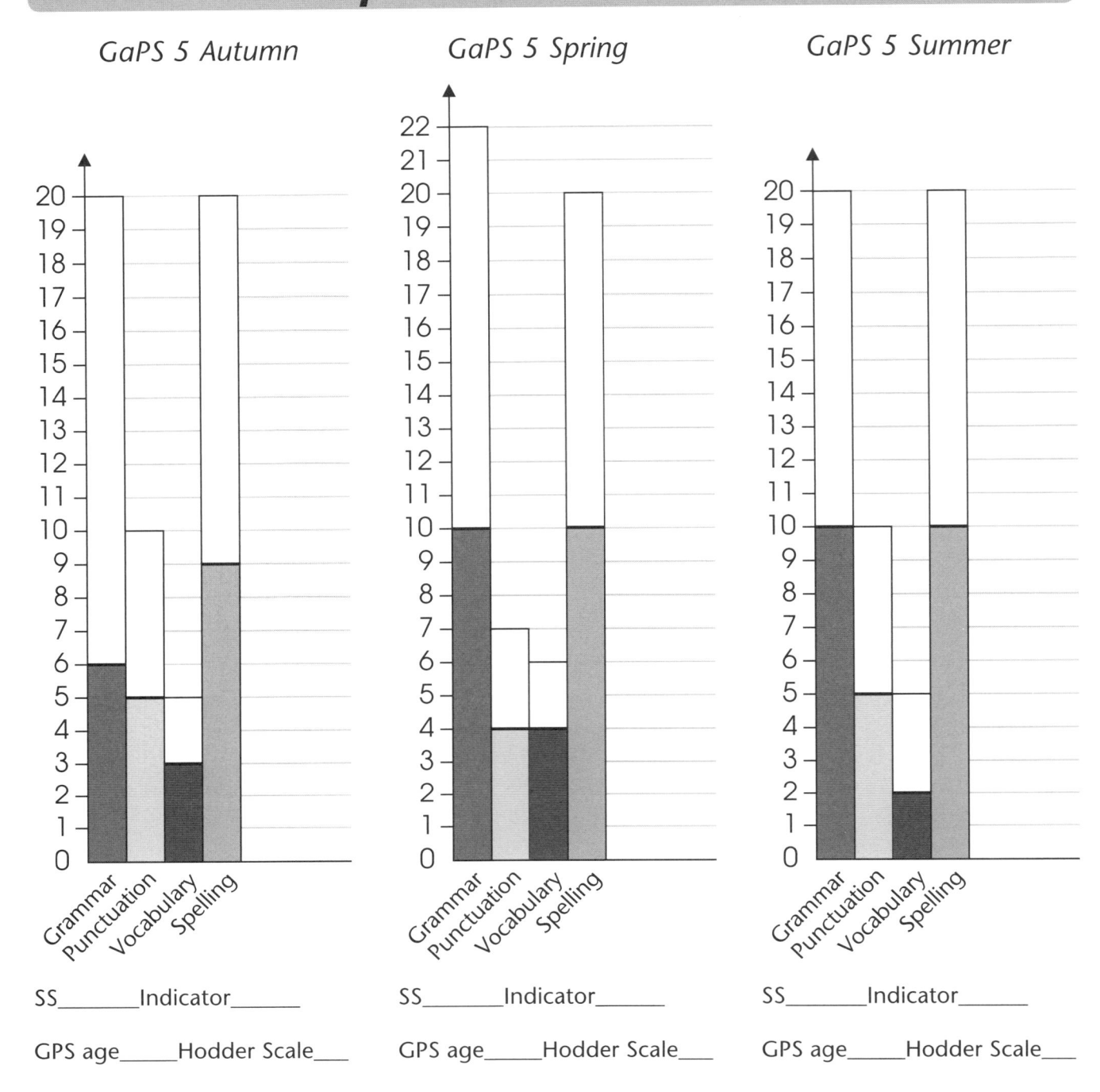

GaPS 5 Autumn

[Bar chart showing: Grammar 6, Punctuation 5, Vocabulary 3, Spelling 9. National averages (tints): Grammar 20, Punctuation 5, Vocabulary 5, Spelling 20.]

SS_____Indicator_____

GPS age_____Hodder Scale___

GaPS 5 Spring

[Bar chart showing: Grammar 10, Punctuation 4, Vocabulary 4, Spelling 10. National averages (tints): Grammar 22, Punctuation 7, Vocabulary 6, Spelling 20.]

SS_____Indicator_____

GPS age_____Hodder Scale___

GaPS 5 Summer

[Bar chart showing: Grammar 10, Punctuation 5, Vocabulary 2, Spelling 10. National averages (tints): Grammar 20, Punctuation 10, Vocabulary 5, Spelling 20.]

SS_____Indicator_____

GPS age_____Hodder Scale___

Note: The tints show the national average scores obtained in the standardisation trial, rounded to whole marks.

© Rising Stars UK Ltd 2018. You may photocopy this page.

108 Record Sheet

gaps Record Sheet
Pupil name ....

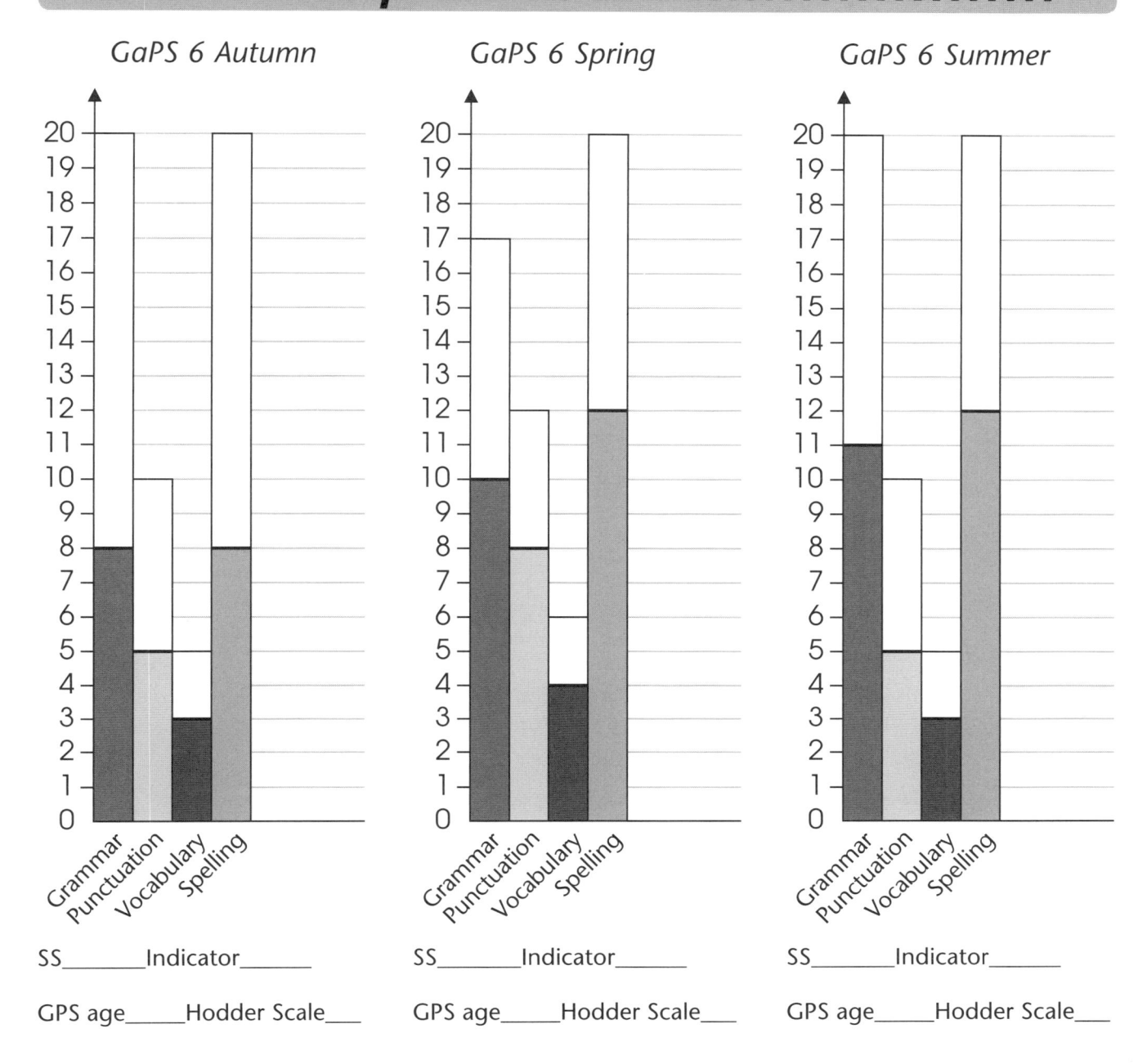

GaPS 6 Autumn

(Bar chart with y-axis 0–20; bars for Grammar, Punctuation, Vocabulary, Spelling)

SS_____Indicator_____

GPS age_____Hodder Scale___

GaPS 6 Spring

(Bar chart with y-axis 0–20; bars for Grammar, Punctuation, Vocabulary, Spelling)

SS_____Indicator_____

GPS age_____Hodder Scale___

GaPS 6 Summer

(Bar chart with y-axis 0–20; bars for Grammar, Punctuation, Vocabulary, Spelling)

SS_____Indicator_____

GPS age_____Hodder Scale___

Note: The tints show the national average scores obtained in the standardisation trial, rounded to whole marks.

© Rising Stars UK Ltd 2018. You may photocopy this page.

4 Test scores

Summative measures

Raw scores

A pupil's raw score is the total mark on a particular test. As an overview, you can evaluate how well a pupil has done by comparing his/her raw score to Table 4.1. This shows average raw scores from our standardisation sample for each *GaPS* test by term and gender. You may also compare your class average raw scores to these averages, as shown in the tables beneath each term's mark scheme.

Table 4.1: Average raw scores for each test by term and gender in the standardisation trial

	Autumn test			Spring test			Summer test		
	Boys	Girls	*Total*	Boys	Girls	*Total*	Boys	Girls	*Total*
GaPS 3	18.9	21.8	20.7	20.5	23.8	22.4	21.6	24.7	23.5
GaPS 4	24.4	25.1	24.4	27.7	28.8	28.6	25.0	25.7	25.9
GaPS 5	22.8	24	23.6	27.0	28.8	28.3	26.8	28.0	27.9
GaPS 6	22.9	25.2	24.3	32.6	34.7	34.0	28.0	30.7	30.2

In addition to raw scores, the results obtained from *GaPS* will also enable you to report pupil performance in terms of:

- age-standardised score (see tables in **Chapter 6**);
- standardised score (see tables in **Chapter 6**);
- percentile (**Table 4.3** on page 113);
- GPS age (**Table 4.4** on page 115);
- performance indicators (see **Table 1.2** on page 9);
- the Hodder Scale; see **Table 4.5** on pages 119–20).

Age-standardised scores, standardised scores and confidence bands

Both types of standardised score obtained from *GaPS* are standardised to a mean score of 100, immediately showing whether a pupil is above or below average as compared to the *GaPS* national standardisation sample. Age-standardised scores can be used to compare how a child is performing against other children of the same age (in months) from the cohort taking the same test. For example, a child who has a *standardised score* of 100 (i.e. who is at the mean average score of the whole cohort that took the test, including both older and younger children), could have a higher *age-standardised score* of, say 110, if that child is above average for their particular age (or the converse).

Standardised scores can be used to compare how a child is performing against all other children taking the same test, that is with other children or schools doing the same test.

Please note that age-standardised and standardised scores are quite different measures and are calculated differently. Therefore it is not appropriate to relate a child's age-standardised score to their standardised score.

Age-standardised scores

There are a number of advantages of using age-standardised scores for comparing summative performance. These include the following:

- They are standardised to an average score of 100, immediately showing whether a pupil is above or below average for their age, relative to the *GaPS'* national standardisation sample.

- They allow comparisons to take into account the pupils' ages: pupils born earlier in the academic year are likely to have higher *raw scores* than younger pupils, but could have a lower *age-standardised score*. This enables you to rank pupils in order of achievement after age has been accounted for. *Note:* With older pupils, exposure to teaching is likely to have a significant if not greater impact on achievement than the chronological age of the child.

By definition, age-standardised scores suggest that older children will do better than younger children. In most tests, that span a number of years, this is indeed the case as age and experience do matter. However, the *GaPS* tests are written for each individual year group and our research found that in some tests age correlated weakly with performance, particularly in the Spring term tests. This is not surprising as the children were all receiving a fairly common experience based on national guidelines. This common experience tended to outweigh the effect of chronological age and we found that progress was weakly linked to age and reflects much more the quality of teaching.

The age-standardised scores provided in Chapter 6 range between 70 and 130, with a mean of 100 and a standard deviation (SD) of 15. The SD tells you how spread out the scores are from the mean.

Using the SD and the 'normal distribution' of scores, pupils can be grouped by performance into bands. Figure 4.1 on page 112 illustrates this grouping:

- Average refers to those whose performance is within one SD either side of the mean, i.e. 85–115.

- Below average and above average refer to those who are between one and two SDs either side of the mean, i.e. 70–85 and 115–130.

For many teachers, the term *average*, based on one SD each side of the mean, is too wide and so they prefer the *higher average* and *lower average* bands that are also shown on Figure 4.1 on page 112 and in Table 4.2 on page 112.

The 90 per cent confidence band for the Key Stage 2 *GaPS* tests is typically plus or minus 4 (see Table 5.2 on pages 125–6) – so for a pupil with an age-standardised score of, for example, 106 you can be 90 per cent confident that their 'true' score is between 102 and 110. This spread is lower than for many tests and indicative of the high reliability of the *GaPS* tests. To obtain an age-standardised score, first calculate the pupil's chronological age in years and completed months and then refer to the conversion tables in Chapter 6. Record this on the front of the test booklet.

Figure 4.1: The normal distribution curve showing standard deviations, standardised and age-standardised scores, and percentiles

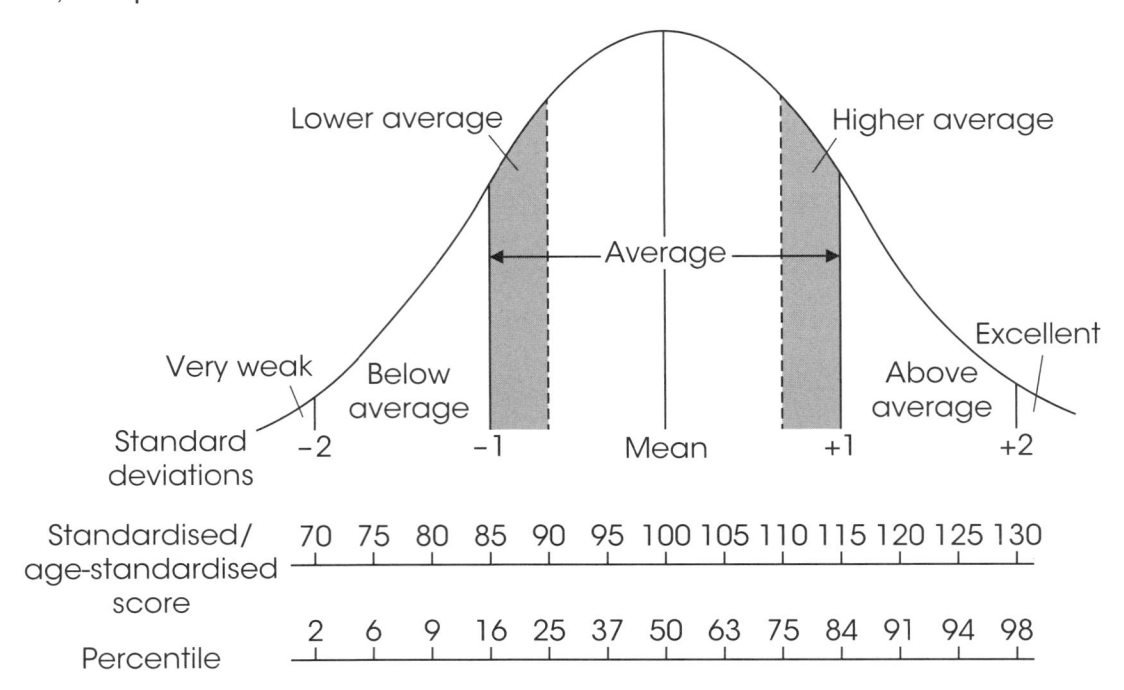

Standardised scores

Standardised scores also have a norm (mean) of 100 and a standard deviation of 15, and in many ways are similar to age-standardised scores, except no allowance is made for the age of the child. As such, much of the above information applies to standardised scores.

We have included, in Chapter 6, standardised scores for all the *GaPS* tests. They are useful for comparing children from one cohort to another but require that the children take the same test for this comparison to be made. The look-up tables provided are based on the performance of the nationally representative sample. A score of 100 is an average score, whichever test the pupil uses. If a pupil gets a standardised score of 100 in Year 2 and they make average progress over the following year, we would also expect them to get a score of 100 in Year 3. If they get higher than 100 they will have made greater than expected progress, compared to our standardisation sample.

Table 4.2: Relationship between age-standardised/standardised test scores and qualitative interpretations

Standardised score	Qualitative interpretation	Standard deviation from mean	Percentile score	Percentage of normal population
>130	Excellent	>+2	>98	2.27
116–130	Above average	+1 to +2	84–98	13.59
110–115 85–115 85–90	*Higher average* Average/age-appropriate *Lower average*	−1 to +1	16–83	68.26
70–84	Below average	−1 to −2	2–15	13.59
<69	Very weak	<−2	<2	2.27

To suggest that one pupil is better than another and to place pupils in order of merit, you must be confident that the score obtained on the test is a reliable score and therefore a true reflection of ability. A 100% reliable score is always unknown because no test can be constructed to provide a perfect reflection of a person's ability. Therefore, tests often use confidence bands for each score to tell you how confident you can be that the score is a true score.

Percentiles

Percentiles can help to give you a better feel for the significance of a pupil's performance, because they show the percentage in each age group who score below a certain level. So an age-standardised or standardised score at the 68th percentile means that 68 per cent of the group scored below that pupil's standardised score. Thus the pupil is in the top third for his/her age group. Percentile scores may be derived from age-standardised scores or raw scores or anything else. To obtain a pupil's percentile, first calculate the pupil's chronological age in years and completed months, obtain his/her age-standardised score using the appropriate conversion table at the end of this manual, and then refer to Table 4.3 below. Equally, standardised scores may be used in the same way but obviously without the need to reference a chronological age. The relationship between standardised or age-standardised scores and percentiles is most easily seen by reference to Figure 4.1 on page 112.

Table 4.3: Conversion of standardised and age-standardised scores to percentiles

Age-standardised score/ Standardised score	Percentile	Age-standardised score/ Standardised score	Percentile	Age-standardised score/ Standardised score	Percentile
≥130	≥98	108	70	89	24
128–9	97	107	68	88	22
126–7	96	106	66	87	20
125	95	105	63	86	18
123–4	94	104	60	85	16
122	93	103	58	84	14
121	92	102	55	83	13
120	91	101	52	82	12
119	90	100	50	81	11
118	89	99	48	80	9
117	87	98	45	79	8
116	86	97	42	78	7
115	84	96	40	76–7	6
114	82	95	37	75	5
113	80	94	34	73–4	4
112	78	93	32	71–2	3
111	77	92	30	70	2
110	74	91	28	<70	1
109	72	90	26		

Grammar, punctuation, vocabulary and spelling ages

Grammar, punctuation, vocabulary and spelling (GPS) ages can be used by teachers as a quick reference: a GPS age shows the *average* chronological age of the pupils who obtained each particular raw score – that is, the chronological age at which this level of performance is typical. However, for more detailed comparative information, and especially for tracking progress over time, age-standardised scores and percentiles are to be preferred.

Note that the GPS ages are provided for ages beyond the normal age range for a given year group. These have been generated by using statistical extrapolations, by up to six months either side of the main range of Key Stage 2 pupils taking the tests in the standardisation. Such extrapolations can be especially useful in interpreting the performance of weaker pupils who have been given a test for a younger age range. To obtain a pupil's GPS age, use Table 4.4 on pages 115–116 and read across from the pupil's raw score to the appropriate column for the test taken. Record this on the front of the test booklet. Alternatively use the tables on page 127 onwards for quick reference.

Table 4.4: GPS ages for each term

Raw score	GaPS 3 Autumn	GaPS 3 Spring	GaPS 3 Summer	GaPS 4 Autumn	GaPS 4 Spring	GaPS 4 Summer	Raw score
1	<6:1	<6:0	<6:6	<6:0	<6:0	<7:0	1
2							2
3							3
4							4
5							5
6							6
7		6:0					7
8		6:2					8
9		6:3					9
10		6:5					10
11		6:6					11
12		6:8		6:0		7:0	12
13	6:1	6:10		6:2		7:2	13
14	6:4	6:11		6:5		7:4	14
15	6:6	7:1		6:7		7:6	15
16	6:9	7:2	6:6	6:9		7:7	16
17	6:11	7:4	6:8	6:11	6:0	7:9	17
18	7:2	7:5	6:10	7:1	6:2	7:11	18
19	7:4	7:7	7:0	7:3	6:5	8:0	19
20	7:6	7:9	7:2	7:6	6:7	8:3	20
21	7:9	7:10	7:4	7:8	6:10	8:4	21
22	7:11	8:0	7:6	7:10	7:0	8:5	22
23	8:2	8:1	7:8	8:0	7:3	8:7	23
24	8:4	8:3	7:11	8:2	7:5	8:9	24
25	8:7	8:4	8:1	8:5	7:8	8:10	25
26	8:9	8:6	8:2	8:7	7:10	9:0	26
27	9:0	8:8	8:5	8:9	8:1	9:2	27
28	9:2	8:9	8:6	8:11	8:3	9:3	28
29	9:5	8:11	8:8	9:1	8:6	9:5	29
30	9:7	9:0	8:10	9:3	8:9	9:7	30
31	>9:7	9:2	9:0	9:6	8:11	9:8	31
32		9:3	9:1	9:8	9:2	9:10	32
33		9:5	9:3	9:10	9:4	10:0	33
34		9:6	9:5	10:0	9:7	10:2	34
35		9:8	9:7	10:2	9:9	10:3	35
36		>9:8	9:9	10:4	10:0	10:5	36
37			9:11	>10:4	10:2	10:7	37
38			10:1		10:5	10:8	38
39			>10:1		10:7	10:10	39
40					10:10	11:0	40
41					>10:10	>11:0	41
42							42
43							43
44							44
45							45

Raw score	GaPS 5 Autumn	GaPS 5 Spring	GaPS 5 Summer	GaPS 6 Autumn	GaPS 6 Spring	GaPS 6 Summer	Raw score
1	<8:2	<8:3	<8:2	<8:8	<8:8	<8:8	1
2							2
3							3
4							4
5							5
6							6
7							7
8							8
9							9
10							10
11							11
12						8:8	12
13	8:2					8:10	13
14	8:4					8:11	14
15	8:5			8:8		9:0	15
16	8:7			8:11		9:2	16
17	8:8			9:1		9:3	17
18	8:10			9:3		9:4	18
19	8:11			9:6		9:6	19
20	9:1	8:3	8:2	9:8		9:7	20
21	9:2	8:6	8:4	9:10		9:8	21
22	9:4	8:8	8:7	10:1		9:10	22
23	9:5	8:11	8:10	10:3		9:11	23
24	9:7	9:1	9:1	10:5	8:8	10:0	24
25	9:8	9:3	9:4	10:7	8:10	10:2	25
26	9:9	9:6	9:7	10:9	9:0	10:3	26
27	9:11	9:8	9:10	11:0	9:2	10:4	27
28	10:0	9:11	10:1	11:2	9:5	10:6	28
29	10:2	10:1	10:4	11:4	9:7	10:7	29
30	10:3	10:4	10:7	11:7	9:9	10:8	30
31	10:5	10:6	10:9	11:9	9:11	10:10	31
32	10:6	10:9	11:0	11:11	10:1	10:11	32
33	10:8	10:11	11:3	12:1	10:3	11:0	33
34	10:9	11:1	11:6	12:4	10:6	11:2	34
35	10:11	11:4	11:9	12:6	10:8	11:3	35
36	11:0	11:6	12:0	12:8	10:10	11:4	36
37	11:2	11:9	12:3	12:10	11:0	11:6	37
38	11:3	11:11	12:6	13:1	11:2	11:7	38
39	11:5	12:2	12:9		11:4	11:8	39
40	11:6	12:4	13:0		11:7	11:10	40
41	11:8	12:6			11:9	11:11	41
42	11:9	12:9			11:11	12:0	42
43	11:11	12:11			12:1	12:2	43
44					12:3	12:3	44
45					12:5	12:4	45
46					12:8	12:6	46
47			>13:0	>13:1	12:10	12:7	47
48	>11:11	>12:11			13:0	12:8	48
49					13:2	12:10	49
50						12:11	50
51						13:0	51
52					>13:2	13:2	52
53						13:3	53
54						>13:3	54
55							55

4 Test scores

Hodder Scale scores

Refer to the tables on page 127–38 to obtain the Hodder Scale score and predicted score for each pupil. This scale is provided as a decimal scale from 0–7 and allows you to monitor the pupils' progress. It is also useful if the pupil falls outside the chronological age range of the age-standardised score table for the test used, because you may still obtain a score on the Hodder Scale.

Diagnostic and formative interpretation

Summative measures are valuable to provide an *overall* picture of the child's performance relative to his/her peers. Such data may, for example, confirm that the pupil is doing well for his/her age and indicate that no intervention strategy is required. However, a more detailed check may show, for example, that good performance in one part of the test is masking poor performance on another area.

Use the *GaPS* profile to look for patterns of strengths and weaknesses

Use the *GaPS* profile on the Record Sheets (pages 106–9) or the version on MARK (the online analysis and reporting tool) to see if there are patterns of strengths and weaknesses in:

- Grammar
- Punctuation
- Vocabulary
- Spelling.

Every pupil has particular strengths and weaknesses that will show up in the *GaPS* profile. When you examine the pupil's answers, you can see when there is a change from correct to incorrect answers and at what level of demand this is occurring. This may alert you to generally weak achievement or perhaps to weakness (or strength) in one specific aspect of the curriculum. This may highlight aspects of grammar, punctuation, vocabulary or spelling which have previously been taught but which have been forgotten or were not understood at the time.

It should be borne in mind when undertaking this form of analysis that performance will naturally reflect recent teaching.

Check a pupil's performance on a specific question

You may also go one stage further and check a pupil's individual performance on a specific question and compare how they have performed relative to other pupils in the same year group. Refer to the mark scheme to see what proportion of pupils in that year group answered each question correctly. This is called the facility and is shown as a percentage: 60 per cent shows that 60 per cent of pupils in the nationally representative sample answered the question correctly. If you wish, you can also average your pupils' scores to create an overall *class* or *cohort* profile. The pattern revealed may inform both teaching and target setting, as it will highlight the areas in which pupils are secure or confident and those that need to be addressed.

Obtaining patterns and predictions of performance

The online analysis and reports will make it easier to automatically pinpoint areas of strength which is explained on page 26.

You are able to monitor progress in the strands and to track pupil progress term by term, plus it provides predictions of future performance and an opportunity to monitor against previous performance (see next section). Predictions of progress can also be obtained from the tables on pages 119–20.

The case studies later in this chapter indicate how this comparative information enables some next steps to be planned. With this more detailed picture, it is possible to implement specific teaching strategies to help both low and high attaining pupils to improve.

Reporting progress using the Hodder Scale

In developing the *GaPs* tests, six cohorts of pupils – totalling more than 6000 pupils – were tracked termly over a full academic year. Using this information it was possible to link pupil performance from term to term and year to year, to identify patterns that provide a firm basis on which to project future performance and establish realistic expectations.

The Hodder Scale score is a most useful monitoring scale, as it shows a decimalised measure of progress and enables teachers to monitor progress term by term, enabling you to predict pupils' future performance and measure whether current progress is what would have been expected. The tables on pages 127–38 provide, for each test, a complete set of reference data for reporting progress in terms of the Hodder Scale score. Read across from the pupil's raw score on a particular test to the Hodder Scale score. Record this score on the front of the test booklet. This will give you the Hodder Scale score the pupil should achieve in any future term.

Predicting future performance with the Hodder Scale

You may wish to set targets for the future and monitor progress over a term or year. This is possible for both individual pupils and whole classes, by drawing on the average performance data of over 1000 pupils in each year group, from term to term and across all the years, in the standardisation sample. The tables on pages 119–20 provide this information.

In Key Stage 2, expected progress is roughly 0.2–0.3 Hodder Scale score every term. Some children do better than this, others less well. In Table 4.5 on pages 119–120 look up the term in which the pupil took the test and follow across to see the predicted Hodder Scale score they should achieve if they follow the progress of an average pupil.

For example, a pupil who starts Key Stage 2 with a Hodder Scale score of 2.8 on the *GaPS 2 Summer* test, and who makes average progress, might be expected to have a Hodder Scale score of 3.7 in the *GaPS 3 Summer* test, and 4.5 in the *GaPS 4 Summer* test – and ultimately to gain 5.7 in *GaPS 6 Summer*. In practice, of course, no pupil is 'average' and progress is rarely completely smooth. In addition, the further ahead one is looking, the more tentative are the predictions one can make (see below). The Hodder Scale, however, does provide a well-founded empirically-based statistical basis for making predictions about performance which can then be modified in the light of actual progress.

Monitoring the difference between the *actual* Hodder Scale score and the *predicted* average Hodder Scale score – for an individual pupil or for a whole class – enables you to see if there is increasing divergence or convergence to normal progress.

Table 4.5: Monitoring and predicting progress on a term-by-term basis

From Summer Year 2 through Years 3 and 4

These tables have been conflated for easy use. If there is no Hodder Scale score for that term this is because this score does not relate to a mark in the test. For scores at the very top and bottom end use the detailed tables on page 127 onwards.

\multicolumn{7}{c	}{Average Hodder Scale score}
GaPS 2 Summer	GaPS 3 Autumn	GaPS 3 Spring	GaPS 3 Summer	GaPS 4 Autumn	GaPS 4 Spring	GaPS 4 Summer
1.5	1.8	2.1	2.3	2.6	2.8	3.1
1.8	2.0	2.3	2.6	2.8	3.1	3.4
1.9	2.2	2.4	2.7	3.0	3.2	3.5
2.0	2.3	2.5	2.8	3.1	3.4	3.6
		2.6	2.9	3.2	3.5	3.7
2.1	2.4	2.7	3.0	3.3	3.6	3.8
2.2	2.5	2.8	3.1	3.4	3.7	3.9
2.3	2.6	2.9	3.2	3.5	3.8	4.0
2.4	2.7	3.0	3.3	3.6	3.9	4.1
2.5	2.8	3.1	3.4	3.7	4.0	4.2
2.6	2.9	3.2	3.5	3.8	4.1	4.3
2.7	3.0	3.3	3.6	3.9	4.2	4.4
2.8	3.1	3.4	3.7	4.0	4.3	4.5
2.9	3.2	3.5	3.8	4.1	4.4	4.6
3.0	3.3	3.6	3.9	4.2	4.5	4.7
3.1	3.4	3.7	4.0	4.3	4.5	4.7
3.2	3.5	3.8	4.1	4.4	4.6	4.8
3.3	3.6	3.9	4.2	4.5	4.7	4.9
	3.7	4.0	4.3	4.5	4.7	4.9
	3.8	4.1	4.4	4.6	4.7	4.9
	3.9	4.2	4.5	4.7	>4.7	
	4.1	4.3	4.5	4.7	>4.7	
	4.3	4.5	4.8	>4.7		
	4.6	4.8	4.9	>4.7		

From Summer Year 4 through Years 5 and 6

			Average Hodder Scale score			
GaPS 4 Summer	GaPS 5 Autumn	GaPS 5 Spring	GaPS 5 Summer	GaPS 6 Autumn	GaPS 6 Spring	GaPS 6 Summer
3.1	3.3	3.5	3.7	3.9	4.1	4.2
3.3	3.5	3.7	3.9	4.1	4.3	4.5
3.4	3.6	3.9	4.1	4.2	4.4	4.6
				4.3	4.5	4.7
3.5	3.7	4.0	4.2	4.4	4.6	4.8
3.6	3.8	4.0	4.2	4.4	4.6	4.8
3.7	3.9	4.1	4.3	4.5	4.7	4.9
3.8	4.0	4.2	4.4	4.6	4.8	5.0
3.9	4.1	4.3	4.5	4.7	4.9	5.1
4.0	4.2	4.4	4.6	4.8	5.0	5.2
4.1	4.3	4.5	4.7	4.9	5.1	5.3
4.2	4.4	4.6	4.8	5.0	5.2	5.4
4.3	4.5	4.7	4.9	5.1	5.3	5.5
4.4	4.6	4.8	5.0	5.2	5.4	5.6
4.5	4.7	4.9	5.1	5.3	5.5	5.7
4.6	4.8	5.0	5.2	5.4	5.6	5.8
4.7	4.9	5.1	5.3	5.5	5.7	5.9
4.8	5.0	5.2	5.4	5.6	5.7	5.9
4.9	5.1	5.3	5.5	5.7	5.8	6.0
5.0	5.2	5.4	5.6	5.8	5.9	6.1
5.1	5.3	5.5	5.7	5.9	6.1	6.2
5.2	5.4	5.6	5.8	6.0	6.2	6.3
	5.5	5.7	5.9	6.1	6.3	6.5
	5.7	6.0	6.1	6.3	6.5	6.7
	6.1	6.3	6.5	>6.3		

Case studies

Case study 1 – Layla (Year 3)

Layla is in Year 3. She is a bright girl but her teacher is concerned that she seems to be underperforming. Layla was given the *GaPS* tests in the Autumn and Spring terms. Her scores were disappointing and below what her teacher expected:

GaPS 3 Autumn		GaPS 3 Spring	
Raw score (max 45)	Standardised score	Raw score (max 45)	Standardised score
16	93	16	91

Layla's Record Sheet and the test analysis available in *GaPS* show that Layla's spelling scores are very low as are the scores for grammar and vocabulary. Layla's scores are strongest for punctuation:

	GaPS 3 Autumn Marks	*GaPS 3 Spring* Marks
Grammar	5/13	5/12
Punctuation	6/8	6/8
Vocabulary	2/4	2/5
Spelling	3/20	3/20
Total	16/45	16/45

The teacher has noticed that Layla can take longer than expected with writing and reading and wonders whether Layla may perhaps have dyslexia. Following testing this is confirmed and support is put in place. Layla's parents are very pleased that the school has picked up this issue and that their daughter's special needs can be properly supported to help her achieve her full potential.

Case study 2 – Alexander (Year 6)

Alexander is a very fluent writer but he is not doing well in his *GaPS* tests which has surprised his teacher, given Alexander's scores for maths and reading in *PUMA* and *PiRA* tests which show that he is working at the expected standard. In Year 5 Alexander's raw scores in the Autumn and Spring *GaPS* tests were 21 and 24, giving him below average standardised scores of 95 and 94.

Alexander's teacher reviews his Record Sheets for these tests and sees that the scores for punctuation are particularly low. He reviews Alexander's *GaPS* test results in the school's tracking system and finds that punctuation was also a weakness in Years 3 and 4. As a result Alexander is put into a small group with three other children who find punctuation difficult so that he can receive targeted support. After a few weeks the teacher can see that Alexander's punctuation has improved in his written work and he expects that this will be reflected in Alexander's test result at the end of the Summer term.

Case study 3 – Megan (Year 4)

Megan is now in Year 4 and has been consistently working below age-related expectations since Year 1. She is capable of reaching age-related expectations but lacks confidence and has had considerable disruptions in her home life. Megan's Record Sheet for the Autumn term shows that she is below average across all the GPS strands in her *GaPS* test. She gained a total raw score of just 18 out of 45 – the average raw score was 24.4 – and she only got 3 marks for spelling out of a possible 20 – the average score was 10.5.

In the Spring term Megan is given targeted support for spelling. The teacher has decided to do this as Megan's records show that she did not pass the phonics test in either Year 1 or Year 2 and Megan is also working below age-related expectations in reading. In the Spring term Megan's *GaPS* test score has improved. It is 25 out of 45 (average score of 28.6) and using MARK her teacher can see that this is down to a better score in spelling (8 out of 20 marks compared to an average of 11.9 marks). Megan is starting to be more confident in class too and is occasionally putting up her hand to answer questions.

By the time Megan sits the *GaPS 4* test in the Summer term she is far more confident than at the start of the year. Her work in class and her books show that she has made considerable progress during the year. Her *GaPS* test scores show that Megan is now very close to the *GaPS* national average and her spelling score has improved considerably:

Strand	Number of marks available	Megan's mark	National average mark
Grammar	13	8	8.16
Punctuation	7	4	4.86
Vocabulary	5	2	2.49
Spelling	20	9	10.42
Total	45	23	25.93

5 Technical information

Standardisation sample

In order for us to have confidence in our statistical analyses it is vital that we have a large enough sample of pupils that sat each test. We aimed for a baseline of around 1000 completed scripts for each year group.

To account for some scripts not being returned or some schools dropping out of the trial we distributed 1500 scripts for each year group across 32 schools. This meant that each school received around 40 scripts on average for each year group.

When it came to return completed scripts there was some drop out, with most of the schools returning fewer scripts than had been sent to them. In most cases the final analysis included approximately 1000 scripts and we were therefore confident that the analyses provided reliable results.

We also looked at how representative the samples were of the population of KS2 pupils on two criteria: disadvantage and performance. This was done using the Edubase schools' database (https://get-information-schools.service.gov.uk/).

We looked at the proportion of disadvantaged pupils in each school which are defined as:

- Those who were eligible for free school meals in the last 6 years or are looked after by the LA for a day or more or who have been adopted from care.

The second criteria regarding the proportion of high performing pupils in the school is defined below:

- Those achieving level 5 or above in reading and maths tests at the end of Key Stage 2 and in writing teacher assessment.

From Edubase we calculated the national average proportion (at a school level) which gave us the proportion of disadvantaged pupils as 0.32 and the proportion of high performing pupils as 0.24.

We then compared our sample to the national average and found that the proportion of disadvantaged pupils was approximately the same (0.32) as the national average and the proportion of high performing pupils (0.23) was also approximately the same as the national average.

Reliability

The reliability of a test indicates whether or not we would get similar results from repeated administrations of the test with similar samples of pupils. An appropriate measure of test reliability for *GaPS* is Cronbach's alpha (α) which measures *internal consistency* reliability. To interpret the value of Cronbach's alpha (the reliability coefficient), rules of thumb are useful. Table 5.1 gives us some useful ranges used in practice.

Table 5.1: Rule of thumb for interpreting Cronbach's alpha values

Range of alpha values	Interpretation
$\alpha \geq 0.9$	Excellent
$0.8 \leq \alpha < 0.9$	Good
$0.7 \leq \alpha < 0.8$	Acceptable
$0.6 \leq \alpha < 0.7$	Questionable
$0.5 \leq \alpha < 0.6$	Poor
$\alpha < 0.5$	Unacceptable

The information for each test is given in Table 5.2 on pages 125–126 and shows that the tests are extremely reliable.

All test scores are subject to some margin of error. This does not mean that a child has been assessed incorrectly, but rather that we are making a statistical estimate of the accuracy of the test as a measuring instrument. There are two ways of reporting this margin of error. One is the 90% (or 95%) confidence band and the other is the standard error of measurement (SEM). Using the confidence band, we can say that we are 90% confident that the child's 'true' score lies in a certain range around the obtained score. The 90 per cent confidence band for Key Stage 2 *GaPS* age-standardised scores is +/–4, as shown in Table 5.2 on pages 125–126. This means, for example, that for a child aged 9:2 (nine years and two months) who obtains a raw score of 23 on the *GaPS 4 Autumn* test and hence a standardised score of 98, we can say with 90 per cent confidence that their 'true' standardised score lies between 94 and 102. The confidence band for each test is presented in Table 5.2 on pages 125–126. The SEM estimates how pupils' scores would be distributed around their true score if they took the test several times. The smaller the SEM the more reliable the score. The SEM for each test is also presented in Table 5.2.

For tests targeting a particular age range, we use a standardisation method based on *percentile norms* – the fundamental principle being that scores at the same percentile rank are comparable. Hence a pupil at, say, the 30th percentile in his/her age group has the same relative ability as a pupil at the 30th percentile in any other age group. The standardisation procedure that we have used for these tests is called the *non-parallel linear regression model*. It is the recognised method for age standardising educational tests.[1]

---

[1] Our basic methodology follows D.G. Lewis (see *Statistical Methods in Education*, University of London Press, 1972, pp. 86–96), with enhancements outlined by I. Schagen (see 'A Method for the Age Standardisation of Test Scores', *Applied Psychological Measurement*, 14, 4, December 1990, pp. 387–93).

Table 5.2: Sample statistics and reliability measures

GaPS 3	Autumn	Spring	Summer
Sample size for age-standardisation	787	795	657
Number of children	1088	1195	1123
Number of boys	443	508	468
Number of girls	436	501	479
Mean mark	20.7	22.4	23.5
Boys mean mark	18.9	20.5	21.6
Girls mean mark	21.8	23.8	24.7
Cronbach Alpha	0.94	0.95	0.95
Pearson coefficient	0.68	0.90	0.80
90% confidence band for mean	(14.9, 26.5)	(16.6, 28.2)	(17.8, 29.2)
Standard Error of Measurement	3.51	3.53	3.49

GaPS 4	Autumn	Spring	Summer
Sample size for age-standardisation	867	960	791
Number of children	1100	1271	1187
Number of boys	457	563	512
Number of girls	445	565	528
Mean mark	24.4	28.6	25.9
Boys mean mark	24.4	27.7	25
Girls mean mark	25.1	28.8	25.7
Cronbach Alpha	0.94	0.94	0.94
Pearson coefficient	0.64	0.75	0.56
90% confidence band for mean	(18.7, 30.1)	(22.8, 34.4)	(20.1, 31.7)
Standard Error of Measurement	3.46	3.53	3.5

GaPS 5	Autumn	Spring	Summer
Sample size for age-standardisation	876	901	980
Number of children	1140	1223	1247
Number of boys	503	566	568
Number of girls	470	516	526
Mean mark	23.6	28.3	27.9
Boys mean mark	22.8	27	26.8
Girls mean mark	24	28.8	28
Cronbach Alpha	0.93	0.93	0.94
Pearson coefficient	0.76	0.64	0.71
90% confidence band for mean	(17.0, 30.2)	(21.6, 35.0)	(21.4, 34.4)
Standard Error of Measurement	4.01	4.09	3.96

5 Technical information

GaPS 6	Autumn	Spring	Summer
Sample size for age-standardisation	868	775	752
Number of children	1021	1038	960
Number of boys	467	465	406
Number of girls	396	426	402
Mean mark	24.3	34	30.2
Boys mean mark	22.9	32.6	28
Girls mean mark	25.2	34.7	30.7
Cronbach Alpha	0.94	0.94	0.95
Pearson coefficient	0.69	0.57	0.72
90% confidence band for mean	(17.6, 31.0)	(27.4, 40.6)	(23.6, 36.8)
Standard Error of Measurement	4.09	4.02	4.03

Validity

Strong *validity* for a test like *GaPS* means that the test addresses the material in the curriculum which the children have studied and been taught. Each test, from Year 1 to Year 6, was written to revise the content from the previous term and assess the content of the term the test is set for ensures that tests taken towards the end of the term are valid, however, the teacher should reassure themself that the content set out in the curriculum map for the term (and previous terms) has been covered. Additionally, the test itself must have high reliability (see pages 123–4) so that the results would be replicated by repeated administrations of the test.

gaps — 6 Standardised score tables

Standardised scores, Hodder Scale scores and GPS ages for *GaPS*

The following tables include the standardised score, the Hodder Scale score, the predicted Hodder Scale score for the next term and the GPS age mapped to the raw score for each test.

GaPS 3 Autumn: Standardised scores, Hodder Scale scores and GPS ages

Raw score	Standardised score	Hodder Scale score	Predicted Hodder Scale score	GPS age
1	70	1.8	2.1	<6:1
2	71	1.8	2.1	<6:1
3	72	1.8	2.1	<6:1
4	74	1.8	2.1	<6:1
5	76	2.0	2.3	<6:1
6	77	2.2	2.4	<6:1
7	79	2.3	2.5	<6:1
8	80	2.4	2.7	<6:1
9	82	2.4	2.7	<6:1
10	83	2.5	2.8	<6:1
11	85	2.6	2.9	<6:1
12	86	2.6	2.9	<6:1
13	88	2.7	3.0	6:1
14	90	2.7	3.0	6:4
15	91	2.8	3.1	6:6
16	93	2.8	3.1	6:9
17	94	2.8	3.1	6:11
18	96	2.9	3.2	7:2
19	97	2.9	3.2	7:4
20	99	3.0	3.3	7:6
21	100	3.0	3.3	7:9
22	102	3.0	3.3	7:11
23	104	3.1	3.4	8:2
24	105	3.1	3.4	8:4
25	107	3.2	3.5	8:7
26	108	3.2	3.5	8:9
27	110	3.2	3.5	9:0
28	111	3.3	3.6	9:2
29	113	3.3	3.6	9:5
30	114	3.4	3.7	9:7
31	116	3.4	3.7	>9:7
32	118	3.4	3.7	>9:7
33	119	3.5	3.8	>9:7
34	121	3.5	3.8	>9:7
35	122	3.6	3.9	>9:7
36	124	3.6	3.9	>9:7
37	125	3.7	4.0	>9:7
38	127	3.8	4.1	>9:7
39	128	3.8	4.1	>9:7
40	130	3.9	4.2	>9:7
41	130	4.1	4.3	>9:7
42	130	4.3	4.5	>9:7
43	130	4.6	4.8	>9:7
44	130	4.6	4.8	>9:7
45	130	4.6	4.8	>9:7

GaPS 3 Spring: Standardised scores, Hodder Scale scores and GPS ages

Raw score	Standardised score	Hodder Scale score	Predicted Hodder Scale score	GPS age
1	71	2.1	2.3	<6:0
2	72	2.1	2.3	<6:0
3	73	2.1	2.3	<6:0
4	75	2.1	2.3	<6:0
5	76	2.1	2.3	<6:0
6	77	2.3	2.6	<6:0
7	79	2.4	2.7	6:0
8	80	2.5	2.8	6:2
9	82	2.6	2.9	6:3
10	83	2.7	3.0	6:5
11	84	2.8	3.1	6:6
12	86	2.8	3.1	6:8
13	87	2.9	3.2	6:10
14	88	2.9	3.2	6:11
15	90	3.0	3.3	7:1
16	91	3.0	3.3	7:2
17	93	3.1	3.4	7:4
18	94	3.1	3.4	7:5
19	95	3.2	3.5	7:7
20	97	3.2	3.5	7:9
21	98	3.2	3.5	7:10
22	100	3.3	3.6	8:0
23	101	3.3	3.6	8:1
24	102	3.3	3.6	8:3
25	104	3.4	3.7	8:4
26	105	3.4	3.7	8:6
27	106	3.5	3.8	8:8
28	108	3.5	3.8	8:9
29	109	3.5	3.8	8:11
30	111	3.6	3.9	9:0
31	112	3.6	3.9	9:2
32	113	3.7	4.0	9:3
33	115	3.7	4.0	9:5
34	116	3.7	4.0	9:6
35	117	3.8	4.1	9:8
36	119	3.8	4.1	>9:8
37	120	3.9	4.2	>9:8
38	122	4.0	4.3	>9:8
39	123	4.0	4.3	>9:8
40	124	4.1	4.4	>9:8
41	126	4.2	4.5	>9:8
42	127	4.3	4.5	>9:8
43	128	4.5	4.8	>9:8
44	130	4.8	4.9	>9:8
45	130	4.8	4.9	>9:8

GaPS 3 Summer: Standardised scores, Hodder Scale scores and GPS ages

Raw score	Standardised score	Hodder Scale score	Predicted Hodder Scale score	GPS age
1	70	2.3	2.6	<6:6
2	70	2.3	2.6	
3	71	2.3	2.6	
4	72	2.3	2.6	
5	74	2.3	2.6	
6	75	2.3	2.6	
7	77	2.3	2.6	
8	78	2.6	2.8	
9	79	2.7	3.0	
10	81	2.8	3.1	
11	82	2.9	3.2	
12	84	3.0	3.3	
13	85	3.0	3.3	
14	86	3.1	3.4	
15	88	3.1	3.4	
16	89	3.2	3.5	6:6
17	91	3.2	3.5	6:8
18	92	3.3	3.6	6:10
19	94	3.3	3.6	7:0
20	95	3.4	3.7	7:2
21	96	3.4	3.7	7:4
22	98	3.5	3.8	7:6
23	99	3.5	3.8	7:8
24	101	3.5	3.8	7:11
25	102	3.6	3.9	8:1
26	103	3.6	3.9	8:2
27	105	3.6	3.9	8:5
28	106	3.7	4.0	8:6
29	108	3.7	4.0	8:8
30	109	3.8	4.1	8:10
31	111	3.8	4.1	9:0
32	112	3.8	4.1	9:1
33	113	3.9	4.2	9:3
34	115	3.9	4.2	9:5
35	116	4.0	4.3	9:7
36	118	4.0	4.3	9:9
37	119	4.1	4.4	9:11
38	120	4.1	4.4	10:1
39	122	4.2	4.5	>10:1
40	123	4.2	4.5	
41	125	4.3	4.5	
42	126	4.4	4.6	
43	128	4.5	4.7	
44	129	4.8	>4.7	
45	130	4.9	>4.7	

6 Standardised score tables

GaPS 4 Autumn: Standardised scores, Hodder Scale scores and GPS ages

Raw score	Standardised score	Hodder Scale score	Predicted Hodder Scale score	GPS age
1	70	2.6	2.8	<6:0
2	70	2.6	2.8	
3	70	2.6	2.8	
4	70	2.6	2.8	
5	70	2.6	2.8	
6	72	2.6	2.8	
7	73	2.6	2.8	
8	75	2.8	3.1	
9	76	3.0	3.2	
10	78	3.1	3.4	
11	80	3.1	3.4	
12	81	3.2	3.5	6:0
13	83	3.3	3.6	6:2
14	84	3.3	3.6	6:5
15	86	3.4	3.7	6:7
16	87	3.4	3.7	6:9
17	89	3.5	3.8	6:11
18	90	3.5	3.8	7:1
19	92	3.6	3.9	7:3
20	93	3.6	3.9	7:6
21	95	3.7	4.0	7:8
22	96	3.7	4.0	7:10
23	98	3.7	4.0	8:0
24	99	3.8	4.1	8:2
25	101	3.8	4.1	8:5
26	102	3.9	4.2	8:7
27	104	3.9	4.2	8:9
28	105	3.9	4.2	8:11
29	107	4.0	4.3	9:1
30	109	4.0	4.3	9:3
31	110	4.1	4.4	9:6
32	112	4.1	4.4	9:8
33	113	4.1	4.4	9:10
34	115	4.2	4.5	10:0
35	116	4.2	4.5	10:2
36	118	4.3	4.5	10:4
37	119	4.3	4.5	>10:4
38	121	4.4	4.6	
39	122	4.4	4.6	
40	124	4.5	4.7	
41	125	4.5	4.7	
42	127	4.6	4.7	
43	128	4.7	>4.7	
44	130	4.7	>4.7	
45	130	4.7	>4.7	

GaPS 4 Spring: Standardised scores, Hodder Scale scores and GPS ages

Raw score	Standardised score	Hodder Scale score	Predicted Hodder Scale score	GPS age
1	70	2.8	3.1	<6:0
2	70	2.8	3.1	
3	70	2.8	3.1	
4	70	2.8	3.1	
5	70	2.8	3.1	
6	70	2.8	3.1	
7	70	2.8	3.1	
8	70	2.8	3.1	
9	70	2.8	3.1	
10	71	2.8	3.1	
11	73	2.8	3.1	
12	74	2.8	3.1	
13	76	3.1	3.4	
14	77	3.2	3.5	
15	79	3.2	3.5	
16	80	3.4	3.6	
17	82	3.5	3.7	6:0
18	83	3.5	3.7	6:2
19	85	3.6	3.8	6:5
20	87	3.6	3.8	6:7
21	88	3.7	3.9	6:10
22	90	3.7	3.9	7:0
23	91	3.8	4.0	7:3
24	93	3.8	4.0	7:5
25	94	3.9	4.1	7:8
26	96	3.9	4.1	7:10
27	97	3.9	4.1	8:1
28	99	4.0	4.2	8:3
29	101	4.0	4.2	8:6
30	102	4.1	4.3	8:9
31	104	4.1	4.3	8:11
32	105	4.1	4.3	9:2
33	107	4.2	4.4	9:4
34	108	4.2	4.4	9:7
35	110	4.3	4.5	9:9
36	112	4.3	4.5	10:0
37	113	4.3	4.5	10:2
38	115	4.4	4.6	10:5
39	116	4.4	4.6	10:7
40	118	4.5	4.7	10:10
41	119	4.5	4.7	>10:10
42	121	4.5	4.7	
43	122	4.6	4.8	
44	124	4.7	4.9	
45	126	4.7	4.9	

6 Standardised score tables

GaPS 4 Summer: Standardised scores, Hodder Scale scores and GPS ages

Raw score	Standardised score	Hodder Scale score	Predicted Hodder Scale score	GPS age
1	70	3.1	3.3	<7:0
2	70	3.1	3.3	
3	70	3.1	3.3	
4	70	3.1	3.3	
5	70	3.1	3.3	
6	71	3.1	3.3	
7	72	3.1	3.3	
8	74	3.1	3.3	
9	75	3.1	3.3	
10	77	3.3	3.5	
11	78	3.4	3.6	
12	80	3.5	3.7	7:0
13	81	3.6	3.8	7:2
14	83	3.7	3.9	7:4
15	84	3.7	3.9	7:6
16	86	3.8	4.0	7:7
17	87	3.9	4.1	7:9
18	88	3.9	4.1	7:11
19	90	4.0	4.2	8:0
20	91	4.0	4.2	8:3
21	93	4.1	4.3	8:4
22	94	4.1	4.3	8:5
23	96	4.1	4.3	8:7
24	97	4.2	4.4	8:9
25	99	4.2	4.4	8:10
26	100	4.3	4.5	9:0
27	102	4.3	4.5	9:2
28	103	4.3	4.5	9:3
29	104	4.4	4.6	9:5
30	106	4.4	4.6	9:7
31	107	4.4	4.6	9:8
32	109	4.5	4.7	9:10
33	110	4.5	4.7	10:0
34	112	4.6	4.8	10:2
35	113	4.6	4.8	10:3
36	115	4.6	4.8	10:5
37	116	4.7	4.9	10:7
38	118	4.7	4.9	10:8
39	119	4.8	5.0	10:10
40	120	4.8	5.0	11:0
41	122	4.9	5.1	>11:0
42	123	4.9	5.1	
43	125	5.0	5.2	
44	126	5.1	5.3	
45	128	5.2	5.4	

GaPS 5 Autumn: Standardised scores, Hodder Scale scores and GPS ages

Raw score	Standardised score	Hodder Scale score	Predicted Hodder Scale score	GPS age
1	70	3.3	3.5	<8:2
2	71	3.3	3.5	<8:2
3	73	3.3	3.5	<8:2
4	74	3.3	3.5	<8:2
5	75	3.3	3.5	<8:2
6	77	3.3	3.5	<8:2
7	78	3.3	3.5	<8:2
8	79	3.5	3.7	<8:2
9	81	3.6	3.9	<8:2
10	82	3.7	4.0	<8:2
11	83	3.8	4.0	<8:2
12	85	3.9	4.1	<8:2
13	86	4.0	4.2	8:2
14	87	4.0	4.2	8:4
15	89	4.1	4.3	8:5
16	90	4.1	4.3	8:7
17	91	4.2	4.4	8:8
18	93	4.2	4.4	8:10
19	94	4.3	4.5	8:11
20	95	4.3	4.5	9:1
21	97	4.4	4.6	9:2
22	98	4.4	4.6	9:4
23	99	4.4	4.6	9:5
24	101	4.5	4.7	9:7
25	102	4.5	4.7	9:8
26	103	4.6	4.8	9:9
27	105	4.6	4.8	9:11
28	106	4.6	4.8	10:0
29	107	4.7	4.9	10:2
30	108	4.7	4.9	10:3
31	110	4.7	4.9	10:5
32	111	4.8	5.0	10:6
33	112	4.8	5.0	10:8
34	114	4.9	5.1	10:9
35	115	4.9	5.1	10:11
36	116	5.0	5.2	11:0
37	118	5.0	5.2	11:2
38	119	5.0	5.2	11:3
39	120	5.1	5.3	11:5
40	122	5.2	5.4	11:6
41	123	5.2	5.4	11:8
42	124	5.3	5.5	11:9
43	126	5.4	5.6	11:11
44	127	5.5	5.7	>11:11
45	128	5.7	6.0	>11:11
46	130	6.1	6.3	>11:11
47	130	6.1	6.3	>11:11
48	130	6.1	6.3	>11:11
49	130	6.1	6.3	>11:11
50	130	6.1	6.3	>11:11
51	130	6.1	6.3	>11:11
52	130	6.1	6.3	>11:11
53	130	6.1	6.3	>11:11
54	130	6.1	6.3	>11:11
55	130	6.1	6.3	>11:11

6 Standardised score tables

GaPS 5 Spring: Standardised scores, Hodder Scale scores and GPS ages

Raw score	Standardised score	Hodder Scale score	Predicted Hodder Scale score	GPS age
1	70	3.5	3.7	<8:3
2	70	3.5	3.7	
3	70	3.5	3.7	
4	70	3.5	3.7	
5	70	3.5	3.7	
6	70	3.5	3.7	
7	71	3.5	3.7	
8	72	3.5	3.7	
9	74	3.5	3.7	
10	75	3.5	3.7	
11	76	3.5	3.7	
12	78	3.7	3.9	
13	79	3.9	4.1	
14	80	4.0	4.2	
15	82	4.0	4.2	
16	83	4.1	4.3	
17	84	4.2	4.4	
18	86	4.2	4.4	
19	87	4.3	4.5	
20	89	4.3	4.5	8:3
21	90	4.4	4.6	8:6
22	91	4.4	4.6	8:8
23	93	4.5	4.7	8:11
24	94	4.5	4.7	9:1
25	95	4.6	4.8	9:3
26	97	4.6	4.8	9:6
27	98	4.7	4.9	9:8
28	100	4.7	4.9	9:11
29	101	4.7	4.9	10:1
30	102	4.8	5.0	10:4
31	104	4.8	5.0	10:6
32	105	4.8	5.0	10:9
33	106	4.9	5.1	10:11
34	108	4.9	5.1	11:1
35	109	5.0	5.2	11:4
36	111	5.0	5.2	11:6
37	112	5.0	5.2	11:9
38	113	5.1	5.3	11:11
39	115	5.1	5.3	12:2
40	116	5.2	5.4	12:4
41	117	5.2	5.4	12:6
42	119	5.3	5.5	12:9
43	120	5.3	5.5	12:11
44	121	5.4	5.6	>12:11
45	123	5.4	5.6	
46	124	5.5	5.7	
47	126	5.6	5.8	
48	127	5.7	5.9	
49	128	6.0	6.1	
50	130	6.3	6.5	
51	130	6.3	6.5	
52	130	6.3	6.5	
53	130	6.3	6.5	
54	130	6.3	6.5	
55	130	6.3	6.5	

GaPS 5 Summer: Standardised scores, Hodder Scale scores and GPS ages

Raw score	Standardised score	Hodder Scale score	Predicted Hodder Scale score	GPS age
1	70	3.7	3.9	<8:2
2	70	3.7	3.9	
3	70	3.7	3.9	
4	70	3.7	3.9	
5	70	3.7	3.9	
6	71	3.7	3.9	
7	73	3.7	3.9	
8	74	3.7	3.9	
9	75	3.7	3.9	
10	77	3.7	3.9	
11	78	3.7	3.9	
12	79	3.9	4.1	
13	80	4.1	4.2	
14	82	4.2	4.4	
15	83	4.2	4.4	
16	84	4.3	4.5	
17	86	4.4	4.6	
18	87	4.4	4.6	
19	88	4.5	4.7	
20	90	4.5	4.7	8:2
21	91	4.6	4.8	8:4
22	92	4.6	4.8	8:7
23	94	4.7	4.9	8:10
24	95	4.7	4.9	9:1
25	96	4.8	5.0	9:4
26	98	4.8	5.0	9:7
27	99	4.8	5.0	9:10
28	100	4.9	5.1	10:1
29	101	4.9	5.1	10:4
30	103	5.0	5.2	10:7
31	104	5.0	5.2	10:9
32	105	5.0	5.2	11:0
33	107	5.1	5.3	11:3
34	108	5.1	5.3	11:6
35	109	5.2	5.4	11:9
36	111	5.2	5.4	12:0
37	112	5.2	5.4	12:3
38	113	5.3	5.5	12:6
39	115	5.3	5.5	12:9
40	116	5.4	5.6	13:0
41	117	5.4	5.6	>13:0
42	118	5.5	5.7	
43	120	5.5	5.7	
44	121	5.6	5.8	
45	122	5.6	5.8	
46	124	5.7	5.9	
47	125	5.8	6.0	
48	126	5.9	6.1	
49	128	6.1	6.3	
50	129	6.5	>6.3	
51	130	6.5	>6.3	
52	130	6.5	>6.3	
53	130	6.5	>6.3	
54	130	6.5	>6.3	
55	130	6.5	>6.3	

GaPS 6 Autumn: Standardised scores, Hodder Scale scores and GPS ages

Raw score	Standardised score	Hodder Scale score	Predicted Hodder Scale score	GPS age
1	70	3.9	4.1	<8:8
2	70	3.9	4.1	
3	71	3.9	4.1	
4	73	3.9	4.1	
5	74	3.9	4.1	
6	75	3.9	4.1	
7	77	3.9	4.1	
8	78	4.1	4.3	
9	79	4.2	4.4	
10	81	4.3	4.5	
11	82	4.4	4.6	
12	83	4.5	4.7	
13	85	4.6	4.8	
14	86	4.6	4.8	
15	87	4.7	4.9	8:8
16	89	4.7	4.9	8:11
17	90	4.8	5.0	9:1
18	92	4.8	5.0	9:3
19	93	4.9	5.1	9:6
20	94	4.9	5.1	9:8
21	96	5.0	5.2	9:10
22	97	5.0	5.2	10:1
23	98	5.0	5.2	10:3
24	100	5.1	5.3	10:5
25	101	5.1	5.3	10:7
26	102	5.2	5.4	10:9
27	104	5.2	5.4	11:0
28	105	5.2	5.4	11:2
29	106	5.3	5.5	11:4
30	108	5.3	5.5	11:7
31	109	5.3	5.5	11:9
32	110	5.4	5.6	11:11
33	112	5.4	5.6	12:1
34	113	5.5	5.7	12:4
35	115	5.5	5.7	12:6
36	116	5.6	5.7	12:8
37	117	5.6	5.7	12:10
38	119	5.6	5.7	13:1
39	120	5.7	5.8	>13:1
40	121	5.8	5.9	
41	123	5.8	5.9	
42	124	5.9	6.1	
43	125	6.0	6.2	
44	127	6.1	6.3	
45	128	6.3	6.5	
46	129	6.3	6.5	
47	130	6.3	6.5	
48	130	6.3	6.5	
49	130	6.3	6.5	
50	130	6.3	6.5	
51	130	6.3	6.5	
52	130	6.3	6.5	
53	130	6.3	6.5	
54	130	6.3	6.5	
55	130	6.3	6.5	

6 Standardised score tables

GaPS 6 Spring: Standardised scores, Hodder Scale scores and GPS ages

Raw score	Standardised score	Hodder Scale score	Predicted Hodder Scale score	GPS age
1	70	4.1	4.2	<8:8
2	70	4.1	4.2	
3	70	4.1	4.2	
4	70	4.1	4.2	
5	70	4.1	4.2	
6	70	4.1	4.2	
7	70	4.1	4.2	
8	70	4.1	4.2	
9	70	4.1	4.2	
10	71	4.1	4.2	
11	72	4.1	4.2	
12	73	4.1	4.2	
13	74	4.1	4.2	
14	76	4.1	4.2	
15	77	4.1	4.2	
16	78	4.1	4.2	
17	79	4.1	4.2	
18	80	4.3	4.5	
19	82	4.4	4.6	
20	83	4.5	4.7	
21	84	4.6	4.8	
22	85	4.7	4.9	
23	87	4.7	4.9	
24	88	4.8	5.0	8:8
25	89	4.9	5.1	8:10
26	90	4.9	5.1	9:0
27	91	5.0	5.2	9:2
28	93	5.0	5.2	9:5
29	94	5.0	5.2	9:7
30	95	5.1	5.3	9:9
31	96	5.1	5.3	9:11
32	98	5.2	5.4	10:1
33	99	5.2	5.4	10:3
34	100	5.3	5.5	10:6
35	101	5.3	5.5	10:8
36	102	5.3	5.5	10:10
37	104	5.4	5.6	11:0
38	105	5.4	5.6	11:2
39	106	5.4	5.6	11:4
40	107	5.5	5.7	11:7
41	109	5.5	5.7	11:9
42	110	5.6	5.8	11:11
43	111	5.6	5.8	12:1
44	112	5.6	5.8	12:3
45	113	5.7	5.9	12:5
46	115	5.7	5.9	12:8
47	116	5.8	6.0	12:10
48	117	5.8	6.0	13:0
49	118	5.9	6.1	13:2
50	120	5.9	6.1	>13:2
51	121	6.1	6.2	
52	122	6.1	6.2	
53	123	6.2	6.3	
54	124	6.3	6.5	
55	126	6.5	6.7	

GaPS 6 Summer: Standardised scores, Hodder Scale scores and GPS ages

Raw score	Standardised score	Hodder Scale score	GPS age
1	70	4.2	<8:8
2	70	4.2	<8:8
3	70	4.2	<8:8
4	70	4.2	<8:8
5	70	4.2	<8:8
6	71	4.2	<8:8
7	72	4.2	<8:8
8	73	4.2	<8:8
9	74	4.2	<8:8
10	76	4.2	<8:8
11	77	4.2	<8:8
12	78	4.2	8:8
13	79	4.2	8:10
14	80	4.5	8:11
15	82	4.6	9:0
16	83	4.7	9:2
17	84	4.8	9:3
18	85	4.8	9:4
19	87	4.9	9:6
20	88	5.0	9:7
21	89	5.0	9:8
22	90	5.1	9:10
23	91	5.1	9:11
24	93	5.2	10:0
25	94	5.2	10:2
26	95	5.3	10:3
27	96	5.3	10:4
28	97	5.3	10:6
29	99	5.4	10:7
30	100	5.4	10:8
31	101	5.5	10:10
32	102	5.5	10:11
33	103	5.5	11:0
34	105	5.6	11:2
35	106	5.6	11:3
36	107	5.6	11:4
37	108	5.7	11:6
38	109	5.7	11:7
39	111	5.8	11:8
40	112	5.8	11:10
41	113	5.8	11:11
42	114	5.9	12:0
43	116	5.9	12:2
44	117	6.0	12:3
45	118	6.0	12:4
46	119	6.1	12:6
47	120	6.2	12:7
48	122	6.2	12:8
49	123	6.3	12:10
50	124	6.5	12:11
51	125	6.7	13:0
52	126	7.0	13:2
53	128	7.0	13:3
54	129	7.0	>13:3
55	130	7.0	>13:3

Age-standardised scores

GaPS 3 Autumn: Age-standardised scores

Raw score	7:1	7:2	7:3	7:4	7:5	7:6	7:7	7:8	7:9	7:10	7:11	8:0	8:1	Raw score
1	Award 69 for all scores in this area													1
2														2
3														3
4	73	72	72	71	71	71	70	70	70					4
5	76	76	75	75	74	74	73	73	72	72	72	71	71	5
6	79	78	78	77	77	76	76	76	75	75	74	74	73	6
7	81	81	80	80	79	79	78	78	77	77	76	76	76	7
8	84	83	83	82	82	81	81	80	80	79	79	78	78	8
9	86	85	85	84	84	83	83	82	82	81	81	80	80	9
10	87	87	86	86	86	85	85	84	84	83	83	82	82	10
11	90	89	88	88	87	87	86	86	85	85	85	84	83	11
12	91	91	90	90	89	89	88	87	87	86	86	86	85	12
13	93	92	92	92	91	90	90	89	89	88	87	87	87	13
14	94	94	93	93	93	92	92	91	91	90	89	89	88	14
15	96	95	95	94	94	93	93	93	92	92	91	91	90	15
16	97	97	96	96	95	94	94	94	93	93	92	92	92	16
17	99	98	98	97	97	96	96	95	94	94	94	93	93	17
18	100	100	99	99	98	98	97	97	96	95	95	94	94	18
19	102	101	101	100	100	99	99	98	98	97	96	96	95	19
20	103	103	102	102	101	101	100	100	99	98	98	97	97	20
21	104	104	103	103	102	102	101	101	100	100	99	99	98	21
22	106	105	105	104	104	103	103	102	102	101	101	100	100	22
23	107	106	106	105	105	104	104	103	103	102	102	102	101	23
24	108	108	107	107	106	106	105	105	104	104	103	103	102	24
25	110	109	109	108	107	107	107	106	106	105	104	104	103	25
26	111	111	110	110	109	108	108	107	107	106	106	105	105	26
27	113	112	112	111	111	110	109	109	108	108	107	107	106	27
28	114	114	113	112	112	111	111	110	110	109	109	108	107	28
29	116	115	115	114	114	113	112	112	111	111	110	110	109	29
30	117	117	116	116	115	115	114	113	113	112	112	111	111	30
31	118	118	118	117	117	116	116	115	115	114	113	113	112	31
32	120	119	119	119	118	118	117	117	116	116	115	115	114	32
33	122	122	121	120	120	119	119	118	118	117	117	116	116	33
34	125	124	123	123	122	121	121	120	119	119	118	118	118	34
35	128	127	126	125	124	124	123	122	122	121	120	120	119	35
36		130	129	128	128	127	126	125	124	124	123	122	122	36
37						130	129	129	128	127	126	125	125	37
38											130	129	128	38
39														39
40														40
41														41
42														42
43														43
44														44
45	Award 131 for all scores in this area													45
	7:1	7:2	7:3	7:4	7:5	7:6	7:7	7:8	7:9	7:10	7:11	8:0	8:1	

Raw score	8:2	8:3	8:4	8:5	8:6	8:7	8:8	8:9	8:10	8:11	9:0	9:1	9:2	Raw score
					Age in years and completed months									
1					Award 69 for all scores in this area									1
2														2
3														3
4														4
5	70	70	70											5
6	73	72	72	72	71	71	70	70	70					6
7	75	75	74	74	73	73	73	72	72	71	71	71	70	7
8	77	77	76	76	76	75	75	74	74	73	73	72	72	8
9	79	79	78	78	77	77	76	76	76	75	75	74	74	9
10	81	81	80	80	79	79	78	78	77	77	76	76	76	10
11	83	82	82	81	81	80	80	79	79	79	78	78	77	11
12	85	84	84	83	83	82	82	81	81	80	80	79	79	12
13	86	86	85	85	84	84	83	83	82	82	81	81	80	13
14	87	87	87	86	86	85	85	84	84	83	83	82	82	14
15	89	89	88	87	87	87	86	86	85	85	84	84	83	15
16	91	90	90	89	89	88	87	87	86	86	86	85	85	16
17	92	92	91	91	90	90	89	89	88	87	87	86	86	17
18	93	93	93	92	92	91	91	90	90	89	88	88	87	18
19	95	94	94	93	93	93	92	92	91	91	90	89	89	19
20	96	96	95	94	94	94	93	93	92	92	91	91	90	20
21	98	97	97	96	95	95	94	94	93	93	93	92	92	21
22	99	99	98	98	97	96	96	95	95	94	94	93	93	22
23	101	100	99	99	98	98	97	97	96	96	95	94	94	23
24	102	101	101	100	100	99	99	98	98	97	96	96	95	24
25	103	103	102	102	101	101	100	100	99	99	98	97	97	25
26	104	104	103	103	102	102	101	101	100	100	99	99	98	26
27	106	105	105	104	104	103	103	102	102	101	101	100	100	27
28	107	107	106	106	105	105	104	103	103	103	102	102	101	28
29	108	108	107	107	106	106	106	105	104	104	103	103	102	29
30	110	110	109	108	108	107	107	106	106	105	105	104	104	30
31	112	111	111	110	110	109	108	108	107	107	106	106	105	31
32	114	113	112	112	111	111	110	110	109	108	108	107	107	32
33	116	115	114	114	113	112	112	111	111	110	110	109	109	33
34	117	117	116	116	115	115	114	113	113	112	112	111	111	34
35	119	118	118	117	117	116	116	116	115	114	114	113	112	35
36	121	120	120	119	119	118	118	117	117	116	116	116	115	36
37	124	123	123	122	121	120	120	119	119	118	118	117	117	37
38	128	127	126	125	124	124	123	122	122	121	120	119	119	38
39			130	129	129	128	127	126	125	124	124	123	123	39
40									130	130	129	128	127	40
41														41
42														42
43														43
44														44
45					Award 131 for all scores in this area									45
	8:2	8:3	8:4	8:5	8:6	8:7	8:8	8:9	8:10	8:11	9:0	9:1	9:2	

GaPS 3 Autumn: Age-standardised scores

GaPS 3 Spring: Age-standardised scores

Raw score	7:5	7:6	7:7	7:8	7:9	7:10	7:11	8:0	8:1	8:2	8:3	8:4	8:5	8:6	Raw score
1					Award 69 for all scores in this area										1
2															2
3	70	70													3
4	75	74	73	72	71	71	70								4
5	79	78	77	76	75	74	73	73	72	71	70				5
6	82	81	81	80	79	78	77	76	75	74	73	72	71	70	6
7	84	83	83	82	81	81	80	79	78	77	76	75	74	73	7
8	86	85	84	84	83	82	82	81	81	79	79	78	77	76	8
9	88	87	86	86	85	84	83	83	82	81	81	80	79	78	9
10	90	89	88	88	87	86	85	84	83	83	82	82	81	80	10
11	91	90	90	89	88	88	87	86	85	84	84	83	82	82	11
12	93	92	91	90	90	89	88	88	87	86	85	84	84	83	12
13	94	94	93	92	91	90	90	89	88	87	87	86	85	84	13
14	96	95	94	93	92	92	91	90	90	89	88	87	86	86	14
15	98	97	96	95	94	93	92	91	91	90	89	89	88	87	15
16	99	98	97	97	96	95	94	93	92	91	91	90	89	88	16
17	100	99	99	98	97	96	95	94	93	93	92	91	90	90	17
18	101	100	100	99	98	98	97	96	95	94	93	92	91	91	18
19	102	101	101	100	99	99	98	97	96	95	94	94	93	92	19
20	103	102	102	101	100	100	99	98	98	97	96	95	94	93	20
21	104	103	103	102	101	101	100	99	99	98	97	96	95	94	21
22	105	104	104	103	102	102	101	100	100	99	98	98	97	96	22
23	106	105	105	104	103	103	102	101	101	100	99	99	98	97	23
24	107	106	105	105	104	104	103	102	102	101	100	100	99	98	24
25	108	107	107	106	105	105	104	103	103	102	101	101	100	99	25
26	109	108	108	107	106	105	105	104	104	103	102	102	101	100	26
27	110	109	109	108	107	107	106	105	105	104	103	103	102	101	27
28	111	110	110	109	109	108	107	106	106	105	104	104	103	102	28
29	113	112	111	110	110	109	108	108	107	106	105	105	104	104	29
30	114	113	112	112	111	110	109	109	108	107	107	106	105	105	30
31	116	115	114	113	112	111	110	110	109	109	108	107	106	106	31
32	117	116	116	115	114	113	112	111	110	110	109	108	108	107	32
33	119	118	117	116	115	115	114	113	112	111	110	110	109	108	33
34	121	120	119	118	117	116	115	115	114	113	112	111	110	110	34
35	122	121	121	120	119	118	117	116	116	115	114	113	112	111	35
36	124	123	122	122	121	120	119	118	118	117	116	115	114	113	36
37	126	125	124	123	123	122	121	120	120	119	118	117	116	115	37
38	130	129	127	126	125	124	123	123	122	121	120	119	119	118	38
39				130	129	128	126	125	124	123	123	122	121	120	39
40							130	128	127	126	124	124	123	40
41												130	129	127	41
42															42
43															43
44															44
45					Award 131 for all scores in this area										45
	7:5	7:6	7:7	7:8	7:9	7:10	7:11	8:0	8:1	8:2	8:3	8:4	8:5	8:6	

Raw score	8:7	8:8	8:9	8:10	8:11	9:0	9:1	9:2	9:3	9:4	9:5	9:6	9:7	Raw score
				Age in years and completed months										
1					Award 69 for all scores in this area									1
2														2
3														3
4														4
5														5
6	70													6
7	72	71	70	70										7
8	75	74	73	72	71	70								8
9	77	76	75	74	73	72	72	71	70					9
10	79	78	77	76	76	75	74	73	72	71	70			10
11	81	80	79	78	77	77	76	75	74	73	72	71	70	11
12	82	82	81	80	79	78	77	77	76	75	74	73	72	12
13	83	83	82	82	81	80	79	78	77	76	75	75	74	13
14	85	84	83	83	82	82	81	80	79	78	77	76	75	14
15	86	85	84	84	83	83	82	81	81	80	79	78	77	15
16	88	87	86	85	84	84	83	82	82	81	80	79	78	16
17	89	88	87	86	86	85	84	83	83	82	82	81	80	17
18	90	89	89	88	87	86	85	84	84	83	83	82	81	18
19	91	90	90	89	88	87	87	86	85	84	83	83	82	19
20	92	91	91	90	89	89	88	87	86	85	84	84	83	20
21	94	93	92	91	90	90	89	88	88	87	86	85	84	21
22	95	94	93	92	92	91	90	89	89	88	87	86	85	22
23	96	95	95	94	93	92	91	90	90	89	88	88	87	23
24	98	97	96	95	94	93	92	92	91	90	89	89	88	24
25	99	98	97	96	96	95	94	93	92	91	90	90	89	25
26	100	99	99	98	97	96	95	94	93	92	92	91	90	26
27	101	100	99	99	98	97	97	96	95	94	93	92	91	27
28	102	101	100	100	99	99	98	97	96	95	94	93	92	28
29	103	102	102	101	100	100	99	98	98	97	96	95	94	29
30	104	103	103	102	101	101	100	99	99	98	97	96	95	30
31	105	104	104	103	102	102	101	100	100	99	99	98	97	31
32	106	105	105	104	104	103	102	102	101	100	100	99	98	32
33	108	107	106	105	105	104	104	103	102	102	101	100	100	33
34	109	108	108	107	106	105	105	104	104	103	102	102	101	34
35	110	110	109	108	108	107	106	105	105	104	104	103	102	35
36	112	111	111	110	109	109	108	107	106	106	105	104	104	36
37	114	113	113	112	111	110	109	109	108	108	107	106	105	37
38	117	116	115	114	113	112	112	111	110	109	109	108	107	38
39	119	119	118	117	116	115	114	113	112	112	111	110	109	39
40	122	121	121	120	119	118	117	117	116	115	114	113	112	40
41	126	125	124	123	122	122	121	120	119	118	118	117	116	41
42				130	129	128	126	125	124	123	123	122	121	120	42
43											130	128	127	43
44														44
45					Award 131 for all scores in this area									45
	8:7	8:8	8:9	8:10	8:11	9:0	9:1	9:2	9:3	9:4	9:5	9:6	9:7	

GaPS 3 Spring: Age-standardised scores

GaPS 3 Summer: Age-standardised scores

Raw score	7:7	7:8	7:9	7:10	7:11	8:0	8:1	8:2	8:3	8:4	8:5	8:6	8:7	8:8	Raw score
1					Award 69 for all scores in this area										1
2															2
3															3
4	71	71	70	70	70										4
5	74	74	73	72	72	71	71	70	70						5
6	77	76	75	75	74	74	73	72	72	71	71	70	70		6
7	79	78	77	77	76	76	75	75	74	73	73	72	72	71	7
8	81	80	79	79	78	78	77	76	76	75	75	74	73	73	8
9	82	82	81	81	80	79	79	78	77	77	76	76	75	75	9
10	84	83	83	82	82	81	80	80	79	78	78	77	77	76	10
11	85	84	84	83	83	82	82	81	81	80	79	79	78	78	11
12	87	86	85	85	84	84	83	82	82	81	81	80	80	79	12
13	88	87	87	86	85	85	84	84	83	83	82	82	81	80	13
14	89	88	88	87	87	86	85	85	84	84	83	83	82	82	14
15	90	89	89	88	88	87	87	86	85	85	84	84	83	83	15
16	91	91	90	89	89	88	88	87	87	86	85	85	84	84	16
17	93	92	91	90	90	89	89	88	88	87	87	86	85	85	17
18	94	93	93	92	91	90	90	89	89	88	88	87	87	86	18
19	95	95	94	93	92	92	91	90	90	89	89	88	88	87	19
20	97	96	95	95	94	93	92	92	91	90	89	89	88	88	20
21	98	98	97	96	95	94	94	93	92	91	91	90	89	89	21
22	100	99	98	97	96	96	95	94	93	93	92	91	90	90	22
23	101	100	99	99	98	97	96	95	95	94	93	92	92	91	23
24	102	101	101	100	99	99	98	97	96	95	95	94	93	92	24
25	103	102	102	101	100	100	99	98	98	97	96	95	94	94	25
26	104	103	103	102	102	101	100	100	99	98	97	96	96	95	26
27	105	104	104	103	103	102	101	101	100	99	99	98	97	96	27
28	107	106	105	104	103	103	102	102	101	101	100	99	99	98	28
29	108	107	107	106	105	104	103	103	102	102	101	101	100	99	29
30	110	109	108	107	107	106	105	104	103	103	102	102	101	101	30
31	111	111	110	109	108	107	107	106	105	104	103	103	102	102	31
32	113	112	111	111	110	109	108	107	107	106	105	104	103	103	32
33	115	114	113	112	112	111	110	109	108	108	107	106	105	104	33
34	117	116	115	114	113	113	112	111	110	109	109	108	107	106	34
35	119	118	117	117	116	115	114	113	112	111	111	110	109	108	35
36	122	121	120	119	118	117	116	115	114	113	113	112	111	110	36
37	125	124	123	122	121	120	119	118	117	116	115	114	113	112	37
38	129	128	126	125	124	123	122	121	120	119	118	117	116	115	38
39				129	128	127	126	125	124	123	122	120	119	118	39
40							130	128	127	126	125	124	123	40
41													129	128	41
42															42
43															43
44															44
45					Award 131 for all scores in this area										45
	7:7	7:8	7:9	7:10	7:11	8:0	8:1	8:2	8:3	8:4	8:5	8:6	8:7	8:8	

Raw score	8:9	8:10	8:11	9:0	9:1	9:2	9:3	9:4	9:5	9:6	9:7	9:8	9:9	9:10	Raw score
					Age in years and completed months										
1					Award 69 for all scores in this area										1
2															2
3															3
4															4
5															5
6															6
7	71	70	70												7
8	72	72	71	71	70	70									8
9	74	73	73	72	72	71	71	70	70						9
10	76	75	74	74	73	73	72	72	71	71	70	70			10
11	77	76	76	75	75	74	73	73	72	72	71	71	70	70	11
12	78	78	77	77	76	75	75	74	74	73	72	72	71	71	12
13	80	79	78	78	77	77	76	75	75	74	74	73	73	72	13
14	81	80	80	79	79	78	77	77	76	75	75	74	74	73	14
15	82	82	81	80	80	79	79	78	77	77	76	75	75	74	15
16	83	83	82	82	81	80	80	79	78	78	77	77	76	75	16
17	84	84	83	82	82	81	81	80	80	79	78	78	77	77	17
18	85	85	84	83	83	82	82	81	81	80	80	79	78	78	18
19	86	86	85	84	84	83	83	82	82	81	81	80	79	79	19
20	88	87	86	86	85	84	84	83	83	82	82	81	81	80	20
21	88	88	87	87	86	85	85	84	84	83	83	82	82	81	21
22	89	89	88	88	87	87	86	85	85	84	84	83	82	82	22
23	90	90	89	89	88	88	87	86	86	85	84	84	83	83	23
24	92	91	90	89	89	88	88	88	87	86	86	85	84	84	24
25	93	92	91	91	90	89	89	88	88	87	87	86	85	85	25
26	94	93	93	92	91	90	90	89	89	88	88	87	87	86	26
27	96	95	94	93	93	92	91	90	90	89	89	88	88	87	27
28	97	96	95	95	94	93	92	92	91	90	90	89	89	88	28
29	99	98	97	96	95	95	94	93	92	92	91	90	89	89	29
30	100	99	99	98	97	96	95	94	94	93	92	91	91	90	30
31	101	101	100	99	99	98	97	96	95	94	94	93	92	91	31
32	102	102	101	101	100	99	99	98	97	96	95	95	94	93	32
33	104	103	103	102	101	101	100	99	99	98	97	96	95	95	33
34	105	104	104	103	103	102	102	101	100	100	99	98	97	96	34
35	107	107	106	105	104	103	103	102	102	101	101	100	99	99	35
36	109	109	108	107	106	105	104	104	103	103	102	102	101	100	36
37	112	111	110	109	108	108	107	106	105	104	104	103	103	102	37
38	114	113	113	112	111	110	109	109	108	107	106	105	104	104	38
39	118	117	116	115	114	113	112	111	111	110	109	108	107	107	39
40	122	121	119	119	118	117	116	115	114	113	112	111	111	110	40
41	127	126	124	123	122	121	120	119	118	118	117	116	115	114	41
42					130	128	127	126	125	124	123	122	120	119	42
43													130	129	43
44															44
45					Award 131 for all scores in this area										45
Raw score	8:9	8:10	8:11	9:0	9:1	9:2	9:3	9:4	9:5	9:6	9:7	9:8	9:9	9:10	Raw score

GaPS 3 Summer: Age-standardised scores

GAPS 4 Autumn: Age-standardised scores

Raw score	8:1	8:2	8:3	8:4	8:5	8:6	8:7	8:8	8:9	8:10	8:11	9:0	9:1	Raw score
1					Award 69 for all scores in this area									1
2														2
3														3
4														4
5	72	71	71	70	70	70								5
6	74	73	73	72	72	72	71	71	70	70				6
7	76	76	75	75	74	74	73	73	72	72	71	71	70	7
8	78	77	77	76	76	76	75	75	74	73	73	72	72	8
9	80	79	79	78	78	77	77	76	76	75	75	74	74	9
10	81	81	80	80	79	79	78	78	77	77	76	76	75	10
11	83	82	82	81	81	80	80	79	79	78	78	77	77	11
12	84	84	83	83	82	82	81	81	80	80	79	79	78	12
13	85	85	84	84	83	83	82	82	81	81	81	80	79	13
14	87	86	86	85	85	84	84	83	83	82	82	81	81	14
15	89	88	87	87	86	85	85	84	84	83	83	82	82	15
16	91	90	89	88	87	87	86	86	85	84	84	83	83	16
17	92	91	91	90	89	88	88	87	86	86	85	84	84	17
18	93	93	92	91	91	90	89	89	88	87	86	86	85	18
19	95	94	94	93	92	91	91	90	90	89	88	87	86	19
20	96	96	95	94	94	93	92	91	91	90	90	89	88	20
21	98	97	97	96	95	94	94	93	92	92	91	90	90	21
22	99	99	98	97	97	96	95	95	94	93	92	92	91	22
23	100	100	99	99	98	97	97	96	95	95	94	93	92	23
24	102	101	100	100	99	99	98	97	97	96	95	95	94	24
25	103	102	102	101	100	100	99	99	98	97	97	96	95	25
26	104	104	103	102	102	101	100	100	99	99	98	97	97	26
27	106	105	104	104	103	102	102	101	100	100	99	99	98	27
28	107	106	106	105	105	104	103	103	102	101	100	100	99	28
29	108	108	107	107	106	105	105	104	103	103	102	101	101	29
30	110	109	109	108	107	107	106	106	105	104	104	103	102	30
31	112	111	110	110	109	108	108	107	106	106	105	104	104	31
32	114	113	112	112	111	110	109	109	108	107	107	106	105	32
33	116	115	114	114	113	112	111	110	110	109	108	108	107	33
34	118	117	116	116	115	114	113	113	112	111	110	109	109	34
35	120	119	118	118	117	116	115	115	114	113	112	112	111	35
36	122	121	120	120	119	118	118	117	116	116	115	114	113	36
37	124	123	123	122	121	121	120	119	119	118	117	117	116	37
38	128	127	125	124	124	123	123	122	121	121	120	119	118	38
39			130	129	128	127	126	125	124	123	123	122	121	39
40								130	129	128	127	126	124	40
41														41
42														42
43														43
44														44
45					Award 131 for all scores in this area									45
	8:1	8:2	8:3	8:4	8:5	8:6	8:7	8:8	8:9	8:10	8:11	9:0	9:1	

Raw score	9:2	9:3	9:4	9:5	9:6	9:7	9:8	9:9	9:10	9:11	10:0	10:1	10:2	Raw score
1					Award 69 for all scores in this area									1
2														2
3														3
4														4
5														5
6														6
7	70	70												7
8	72	71	71	70	70									8
9	73	73	72	72	71	71	70	70	70					9
10	75	74	74	73	73	72	72	71	71	70	70	70		10
11	76	76	75	75	74	74	73	73	72	72	71	71	70	11
12	78	77	77	76	76	75	75	74	74	73	73	72	72	12
13	79	78	78	77	77	76	76	75	75	74	74	73	73	13
14	80	80	79	79	78	78	77	77	76	76	75	75	74	14
15	81	81	80	80	79	79	78	78	77	77	76	76	75	15
16	82	82	82	81	81	80	79	79	78	78	77	77	76	16
17	84	83	83	82	82	81	81	80	80	79	79	78	78	17
18	85	84	84	83	83	82	82	81	81	80	80	79	79	18
19	86	85	85	84	84	83	83	82	82	81	81	80	80	19
20	87	87	86	85	85	84	84	83	83	82	82	81	81	20
21	89	88	87	87	86	85	85	84	84	83	83	82	82	21
22	90	90	89	88	87	87	86	85	85	84	84	83	83	22
23	92	91	90	90	89	88	87	87	86	85	85	84	84	23
24	93	92	92	91	90	90	89	88	87	87	86	86	85	24
25	95	94	93	92	92	91	91	90	89	88	87	87	86	25
26	96	95	95	94	93	92	92	91	91	90	89	88	87	26
27	98	97	96	96	95	94	93	93	92	91	91	90	89	27
28	99	98	98	97	96	96	95	94	94	93	92	91	91	28
29	100	99	99	98	98	97	96	96	95	94	94	93	92	29
30	102	101	100	100	99	99	98	97	97	96	95	95	94	30
31	103	103	102	101	100	100	99	99	98	98	97	96	96	31
32	105	104	103	103	102	101	101	100	99	99	98	98	97	32
33	106	106	105	104	104	103	103	102	101	100	100	99	99	33
34	108	107	107	106	106	105	104	104	103	102	102	101	100	34
35	110	109	109	108	107	107	106	106	105	104	104	103	102	35
36	113	112	111	110	109	109	108	107	107	106	106	105	104	36
37	115	114	114	113	112	111	110	110	109	108	108	107	106	37
38	118	117	116	116	115	114	113	113	112	111	110	110	109	38
39	121	120	119	119	118	117	116	116	115	114	114	113	112	39
40	124	123	123	122	121	121	120	119	118	118	117	116	116	40
41	130	129	128	126	125	124	124	123	122	122	121	120	120	41
42								130	129	128	127	126	124	42
43														43
44														44
45					Award 131 for all scores in this area									45
	9:2	9:3	9:4	9:5	9:6	9:7	9:8	9:9	9:10	9:11	10:0	10:1	10:2	

GAPS 4 Autumn: Age-standardised scores

GAPS 4 Spring: Age-standardised scores

Raw score	8:5	8:6	8:7	8:8	8:9	8:10	8:11	9:0	9:1	9:2	9:3	9:4	9:5	9:6	Raw score
1						Award 69 for all scores in this area									1
2															2
3															3
4															4
5															5
6															6
7															7
8	71	70													8
9	73	73	72	71	71	70									9
10	76	75	74	74	73	72	72	71	70	70					10
11	77	77	76	76	75	74	74	73	72	72	71	70	70		11
12	78	78	78	77	77	76	76	75	75	74	73	72	72	71	12
13	80	79	79	78	78	77	77	77	76	76	75	74	74	73	13
14	81	81	80	80	79	79	78	78	77	77	76	76	76	75	14
15	83	82	82	81	81	80	80	79	79	78	78	77	77	76	15
16	84	84	83	83	82	81	81	80	80	79	79	78	78	78	16
17	85	85	84	84	83	83	82	82	81	81	80	80	79	79	17
18	86	86	86	85	85	84	84	83	83	82	81	81	80	80	18
19	88	87	87	86	86	85	85	84	84	83	83	82	82	81	19
20	89	88	88	87	87	86	86	85	85	85	84	84	83	82	20
21	90	89	89	88	88	87	87	87	86	86	85	85	84	84	21
22	91	91	90	90	89	89	88	88	87	87	86	86	85	85	22
23	92	92	91	91	90	90	89	89	88	88	87	87	86	86	23
24	94	93	93	92	92	91	91	90	89	89	88	88	87	87	24
25	95	95	94	93	93	92	92	91	91	90	90	89	89	88	25
26	97	96	95	95	94	94	93	93	92	91	91	90	90	89	26
27	98	98	97	96	96	95	95	94	93	93	92	92	91	91	27
28	100	99	98	98	97	97	96	95	95	94	94	93	92	92	28
29	101	100	100	99	99	98	98	97	96	96	95	95	94	93	29
30	102	102	101	101	100	100	99	99	98	97	97	96	95	95	30
31	104	103	103	102	102	101	101	100	99	99	98	98	97	96	31
32	105	105	104	104	103	103	102	102	101	100	100	99	99	98	32
33	108	107	106	105	105	104	104	103	103	102	102	101	100	100	33
34	110	109	108	108	107	106	105	105	104	104	103	103	102	102	34
35	111	111	110	110	109	109	108	107	106	106	105	104	104	103	35
36	113	113	112	112	111	111	110	109	109	108	108	107	106	105	36
37	116	115	115	114	113	113	112	112	111	110	110	109	109	108	37
38	118	118	117	117	116	115	115	114	113	113	112	112	111	111	38
39	121	120	120	119	119	118	118	117	116	116	115	115	114	113	39
40	124	123	123	122	122	121	121	120	119	119	118	118	117	117	40
41	128	128	127	126	125	125	124	124	123	123	122	122	121	120	41
42							130	129	129	128	127	126	125	125	42
43															43
44															44
45						Award 131 for all scores in this area									45
	8:5	8:6	8:7	8:8	8:9	8:10	8:11	9:0	9:1	9:2	9:3	9:4	9:5	9:6	

Raw score	9:7	9:8	9:9	9:10	9:11	10:0	10:1	10:2	10:3	10:4	10:5	10:6	10:7	Raw score
1					Award 69 for all scores in this area									1
2														2
3														3
4														4
5														5
6														6
7														7
8														8
9														9
10														10
11														11
12	71	70												12
13	72	72	71	70	70									13
14	74	74	73	72	72	71	70	70						14
15	76	75	75	74	73	73	72	71	71	70				15
16	77	77	76	76	75	75	74	73	72	72	71	71	70	16
17	78	78	77	77	76	76	75	75	74	74	73	72	72	17
18	79	79	78	78	78	77	77	76	76	75	75	74	73	18
19	81	80	80	79	79	78	78	77	77	76	76	75	75	19
20	82	81	81	80	80	79	79	78	78	77	77	77	76	20
21	83	83	82	82	81	80	80	80	79	79	78	78	77	21
22	84	84	83	83	82	82	81	81	80	80	79	79	78	22
23	86	85	85	84	84	83	82	82	81	81	80	80	79	23
24	87	86	86	85	85	84	84	83	83	82	82	81	81	24
25	88	87	87	86	86	85	85	84	84	83	83	82	82	25
26	89	88	88	87	87	86	86	86	85	85	84	84	83	26
27	90	90	89	89	88	88	87	87	86	86	85	85	84	27
28	91	91	90	90	89	89	88	88	87	87	86	86	85	28
29	93	92	92	91	91	90	90	89	89	88	88	87	87	29
30	94	94	93	93	92	91	91	90	90	89	89	88	88	30
31	96	95	95	94	94	93	92	92	91	91	90	90	89	31
32	98	97	96	96	95	95	94	93	93	92	92	91	91	32
33	99	99	98	97	97	96	96	95	94	94	93	93	92	33
34	101	100	100	99	99	98	98	97	96	96	95	95	94	34
35	103	102	102	101	101	100	99	99	98	98	97	96	96	35
36	105	104	104	103	102	102	101	101	100	100	99	99	98	36
37	107	107	106	105	105	104	103	103	102	102	101	101	100	37
38	110	109	109	108	108	107	106	105	105	104	104	103	103	38
39	113	112	112	111	110	110	109	109	108	107	107	106	105	39
40	116	115	115	114	114	113	112	112	111	111	110	110	109	40
41	120	119	119	118	118	117	116	116	115	115	114	113	113	41
42	124	124	123	123	122	122	121	121	120	119	119	118	118	42
43				130	130	129	128	127	127	126	125	124	124	43
44														44
45					Award 131 for all scores in this area									45
	9:7	9:8	9:9	9:10	9:11	10:0	10:1	10:2	10:3	10:4	10:5	10:6	10:7	

GAPS 4 Spring: Age-standardised scores

GAPS 4 Summer: Age-standardised scores

Raw score	8:7	8:8	8:9	08:10	08:11	9:0	9:1	9:2	9:3	9:4	9:5	9:6	9:7	9:8	Raw score
1						Award 69 for all scores in this area									1
2															2
3															3
4															4
5	70														5
6	72	72	71	70	70										6
7	75	74	73	73	72	71	70	70							7
8	77	77	76	75	74	73	72	72	71	70					8
9	80	79	78	77	76	75	74	74	73	72	71	71	70		9
10	82	81	80	79	78	77	76	76	75	74	73	72	72	71	10
11	83	83	82	81	80	79	78	78	77	76	75	74	73	72	11
12	85	84	83	83	82	81	80	79	78	78	77	76	75	74	12
13	86	85	85	84	83	83	82	81	80	79	78	78	77	76	13
14	87	87	86	85	85	84	83	82	82	81	80	79	78	77	14
15	89	88	87	86	86	85	85	84	83	82	82	81	80	79	15
16	90	89	88	88	87	86	86	85	84	84	83	82	81	81	16
17	92	91	90	89	88	87	87	86	85	85	84	83	83	82	17
18	93	92	91	90	90	89	88	87	86	86	85	85	84	83	18
19	95	94	93	92	91	90	89	88	88	87	86	86	85	84	19
20	96	95	95	94	93	92	91	90	89	88	87	87	86	85	20
21	97	97	96	95	94	93	92	91	90	89	89	88	87	86	21
22	98	97	97	96	96	95	94	93	92	91	90	89	88	87	22
23	99	98	98	97	97	96	95	94	93	92	91	90	89	89	23
24	101	100	99	98	97	97	96	96	95	94	93	92	91	90	24
25	102	101	100	99	98	98	97	97	96	95	95	93	92	91	25
26	103	102	101	101	100	99	98	97	97	96	96	95	94	93	26
27	104	103	102	102	101	100	100	98	98	97	97	96	96	95	27
28	105	104	104	103	102	101	101	100	99	98	98	97	97	96	28
29	106	105	105	104	103	103	102	101	101	100	99	98	97	97	29
30	107	106	106	105	105	104	103	102	102	101	100	100	98	98	30
31	108	108	107	106	106	105	104	104	103	102	102	101	100	99	31
32	110	109	108	108	107	106	106	105	104	104	103	102	102	101	32
33	112	111	110	109	108	107	107	106	106	105	104	104	103	102	33
34	114	113	112	111	110	109	108	108	107	106	106	105	104	104	34
35	115	115	114	113	112	111	110	109	108	108	107	106	106	105	35
36	117	117	116	115	114	113	113	112	110	109	109	108	107	107	36
37	120	119	118	117	116	115	115	114	113	112	111	110	109	108	37
38	122	121	120	119	119	118	117	116	115	115	114	113	112	111	38
39	125	124	123	122	121	121	120	119	118	117	116	115	115	114	39
40		129	128	126	124	124	123	122	121	120	119	118	118	117	40
41						130	128	127	125	124	123	122	121	120	41
42												129	127	126	42
43															43
44															44
45						Award 131 for all scores in this area									45
	8:7	8:8	8:9	08:10	08:11	9:0	9:1	9:2	9:3	9:4	9:5	9:6	9:7	9:8	

Raw score	9:9	9:10	9:11	10:00	10:01	10:02	10:3	10:04	10:5	10:6	10:7	10:8	10:09	10:10	Raw score
					Age in years and completed months										
1					Award 69 for all scores in this area										1
2															2
3															3
4															4
5															5
6															6
7															7
8															8
9															9
10	70														10
11	72	71	70	70											11
12	73	73	72	71	70	70									12
13	75	74	73	73	72	71	70	70							13
14	77	76	75	74	73	72	72	71	70						14
15	78	77	76	75	75	74	73	72	71	71	70				15
16	80	79	78	77	76	75	74	74	73	72	71	71	70		16
17	81	80	79	78	78	77	76	75	74	73	73	72	71	70	17
18	82	82	81	80	79	78	77	76	76	75	74	73	72	72	18
19	84	83	82	81	81	80	79	78	77	76	75	74	74	73	19
20	85	84	83	83	82	81	80	79	78	77	77	76	75	74	20
21	86	85	84	84	83	82	81	81	80	79	78	77	76	75	21
22	87	86	85	85	84	83	83	82	81	80	79	78	78	77	22
23	88	87	86	86	85	85	84	83	82	82	81	80	79	78	23
24	89	88	87	87	86	86	85	84	83	83	82	81	80	80	24
25	90	90	89	88	87	87	86	85	85	84	83	82	82	81	25
26	92	91	90	89	88	88	87	86	86	85	84	84	83	82	26
27	94	93	92	91	90	89	88	87	87	86	85	85	84	83	27
28	95	94	93	92	91	90	89	89	88	87	86	86	85	85	28
29	96	96	95	94	93	92	91	90	89	88	87	87	86	86	29
30	97	97	96	96	95	94	93	92	91	90	89	88	87	87	30
31	98	98	97	97	96	95	95	94	92	91	90	90	89	88	31
32	100	99	98	98	97	97	96	95	94	93	92	91	90	89	32
33	101	101	100	99	98	98	97	97	96	95	94	93	92	91	33
34	103	102	102	101	100	99	98	98	97	97	96	95	94	93	34
35	104	104	103	102	102	101	100	99	98	98	97	97	96	95	35
36	106	105	105	104	103	103	102	101	101	100	99	98	97	97	36
37	108	107	106	106	105	104	104	103	102	102	101	100	99	98	37
38	110	109	108	107	107	106	106	105	104	104	103	102	101	101	38
39	113	112	111	110	109	108	108	107	106	106	105	104	104	103	39
40	116	115	114	114	113	112	110	110	109	108	107	107	106	105	40
41	120	119	118	117	116	115	115	114	113	112	111	110	109	108	41
42	124	123	123	122	121	120	119	118	117	117	116	115	114	113	42
43					130	128	126	125	124	123	122	121	120	120	43
44															44
45					Award 131 for all scores in this area										45
	9:9	9:10	9:11	10:00	10:01	10:02	10:3	10:04	10:5	10:6	10:7	10:8	10:09	10:10	

GAPS 4 Summer: Age-standardised scores

GAPS 5 Autumn: Age-standardised scores

Raw score	9:1	9:2	9:3	9:4	9:5	9:6	9:7	9:8	9:9	9:10	9:11	10:0	10:1	10:2	Raw score
1					Award 69 for all scores in this area										1
2															2
3															3
4															4
5	72	71	71	70	70										5
6	75	75	74	73	73	72	72	71	71	70	70				6
7	78	77	77	76	76	75	75	74	73	73	72	72	71	71	7
8	80	79	79	78	78	77	77	76	76	75	75	74	74	73	8
9	82	82	81	81	80	79	79	78	78	77	77	76	76	75	9
10	85	84	83	83	82	81	81	80	80	79	79	78	77	77	10
11	86	86	85	85	84	84	83	82	82	81	80	80	79	79	11
12	87	87	86	86	86	85	85	84	84	83	82	82	81	80	12
13	89	88	88	87	87	86	86	85	85	85	84	84	83	82	13
14	90	90	89	88	88	87	87	87	86	86	85	85	85	84	14
15	91	91	90	90	89	89	88	88	87	87	86	86	86	85	15
16	93	92	92	91	91	90	90	89	89	88	87	87	87	86	16
17	95	94	93	93	92	91	91	90	90	89	89	88	88	87	17
18	96	95	95	94	93	93	92	92	91	91	90	89	89	88	18
19	97	96	96	95	95	94	94	93	92	92	91	91	90	90	19
20	98	98	97	97	96	95	95	94	94	93	92	92	91	91	20
21	100	99	98	98	97	97	96	96	95	94	94	93	93	92	21
22	101	100	100	99	98	98	97	97	96	96	95	95	94	93	22
23	102	102	101	101	100	99	98	98	97	97	96	96	95	95	23
24	104	103	102	102	101	101	100	99	99	98	97	97	96	96	24
25	105	104	104	103	102	102	101	101	100	99	99	98	97	97	25
26	106	105	105	104	104	103	102	102	101	101	100	99	99	98	26
27	107	106	106	105	105	104	104	103	102	102	101	101	100	99	27
28	108	107	107	106	106	105	105	104	104	103	102	102	101	101	28
29	109	108	108	107	107	106	106	105	105	104	104	103	102	102	29
30	110	110	109	108	108	107	107	106	106	105	105	104	104	103	30
31	112	111	111	110	109	109	108	107	107	106	106	105	105	104	31
32	113	112	112	111	111	110	109	109	108	107	107	106	106	105	32
33	114	114	113	112	112	111	111	110	109	109	108	107	107	106	33
34	116	115	114	114	113	113	112	111	111	110	109	109	108	107	34
35	117	116	116	115	114	114	113	113	112	111	111	110	109	109	35
36	119	118	117	117	116	115	115	114	113	113	112	111	111	110	36
37	120	119	119	118	117	117	116	115	115	114	114	113	112	112	37
38	122	122	121	120	119	118	118	117	116	116	115	114	114	113	38
39	124	124	123	122	121	120	119	119	118	117	117	116	115	115	39
40	127	126	125	124	123	122	121	121	120	119	118	118	117	116	40
41	130	129	128	127	126	124	124	123	122	121	120	119	119	118	41
42				130	129	128	127	125	124	123	123	122	121	120	42
43						130	129	128	126	125	124	123	122		43
44								130	129	128	126	125			44
45											130	129			45
46															46
47															47
48															48
49															49
50															50
51															51
52															52
53															53
54															54
55						Award 131 for all scores in this area									55
	9:1	9:2	9:3	9:4	9:5	9:6	9:7	9:8	9:9	9:10	9:11	10:0	10:1	10:2	

Raw score	10:3	10:4	10:5	10:6	10:7	10:8	10:9	10:10	10:11	11:0	11:1	11:2	11:3	Raw score
					Age in years and completed months									
1					Award 69 for all scores in this area									1
2														2
3														3
4														4
5														5
6														6
7	70	70												7
8	72	72	71	71	70	70								8
9	75	74	73	73	72	72	71	71	70	70				9
10	76	76	76	75	74	74	73	73	72	72	71	70	70	10
11	78	78	77	77	76	76	75	74	74	73	73	72	72	11
12	80	79	79	78	78	77	77	76	76	75	75	74	73	12
13	82	81	80	80	79	79	78	78	77	77	76	76	75	13
14	83	83	82	81	81	80	80	79	78	78	77	77	76	14
15	85	84	84	83	82	82	81	80	80	79	79	78	78	15
16	86	85	85	85	84	83	83	82	81	81	80	80	79	16
17	87	86	86	86	85	85	84	84	83	82	82	81	80	17
18	88	87	87	86	86	86	85	85	85	84	83	83	82	18
19	89	88	88	87	87	87	86	86	85	85	85	84	83	19
20	90	90	89	89	88	88	87	87	86	86	85	85	85	20
21	91	91	90	90	89	89	88	88	87	87	86	86	86	21
22	93	92	91	91	90	90	89	89	88	88	87	87	86	22
23	94	93	93	92	91	91	90	90	89	89	88	88	87	23
24	95	95	94	93	93	92	92	91	90	90	89	89	88	24
25	96	96	95	95	94	93	93	92	92	91	90	90	89	25
26	97	97	96	96	95	95	94	93	93	92	92	91	90	26
27	99	98	97	97	96	96	95	95	94	93	93	92	92	27
28	100	99	99	98	97	97	96	96	95	95	94	93	93	28
29	101	101	100	99	99	98	97	97	96	96	95	95	94	29
30	102	102	101	101	100	99	99	98	97	97	96	96	95	30
31	104	103	102	102	101	101	100	99	99	98	97	97	96	31
32	105	104	104	103	102	102	101	101	100	99	99	98	97	32
33	106	105	105	104	104	103	102	102	101	101	100	99	99	33
34	107	106	106	105	105	104	104	103	103	102	101	101	100	34
35	108	108	107	106	106	105	105	104	104	103	103	102	101	35
36	110	109	108	108	107	107	106	106	105	104	104	103	103	36
37	111	110	110	109	108	108	107	107	106	106	105	105	104	37
38	112	112	111	111	110	109	109	108	107	107	106	106	105	38
39	114	113	113	112	111	111	110	110	109	108	108	107	107	39
40	115	115	114	114	113	112	112	111	111	110	109	109	108	40
41	117	117	116	115	115	114	113	113	112	112	111	110	110	41
42	119	118	118	117	116	116	115	114	114	113	113	112	111	42
43	122	121	120	119	118	118	117	116	116	115	114	114	113	43
44	124	123	122	122	121	120	119	118	118	117	116	116	115	44
45	128	127	125	124	124	123	122	121	120	119	119	118	117	45
46			130	129	127	126	125	124	123	122	121	121	120	46
47							130	128	127	126	125	124	123	47
48										130	129	128		48
49														49
50														50
51														51
52														52
53														53
54														54
55					Award 131 for all scores in this area									55
	10:3	10:4	10:5	10:6	10:7	10:8	10:9	10:10	10:11	11:0	11:1	11:2	11:3	

GAPS 5 Autumn: Age-standardised scores

GAPS 5 Spring: Age-standardised scores

Raw score	9:5	9:6	9:7	9:8	9:9	9:10	9:11	10:0	10:1	10:2	10:3	10:4	10:5	10:6	Raw score
1						Award 69 for all scores in this area									1
2															2
3															3
4															4
5															5
6															6
7															7
8	71	71	70	70											8
9	74	73	73	72	72	71	71	70	70						9
10	76	76	75	75	74	74	73	73	72	71	71	70	70		10
11	78	77	77	77	76	76	75	75	74	74	73	73	72	72	11
12	79	79	79	78	78	77	77	77	76	76	75	75	74	74	12
13	81	81	80	80	79	79	78	78	78	77	77	76	76	76	13
14	82	82	82	81	81	80	80	80	79	79	78	78	77	77	14
15	84	83	83	83	82	82	81	81	81	80	80	79	79	78	15
16	86	85	84	84	84	83	83	82	82	81	81	81	80	80	16
17	87	87	86	86	85	84	84	84	83	83	82	82	82	81	17
18	89	88	88	87	87	86	86	85	84	84	84	83	83	82	18
19	90	89	89	89	88	88	87	87	86	86	85	84	84	84	19
20	92	91	90	90	89	89	89	88	88	87	87	86	85	85	20
21	93	93	92	91	91	90	90	89	89	88	88	88	87	87	21
22	94	94	93	93	92	92	91	91	90	90	89	89	88	88	22
23	95	95	95	94	94	93	93	92	92	91	90	90	89	89	23
24	97	96	96	95	95	95	94	94	93	93	92	91	91	90	24
25	98	97	97	96	96	96	95	95	94	94	93	93	92	92	25
26	99	99	98	98	97	97	96	96	95	95	95	94	94	93	26
27	101	100	100	99	98	98	97	97	97	96	96	95	95	94	27
28	102	101	101	100	100	99	99	98	98	97	97	96	96	95	28
29	103	103	102	102	101	101	100	100	99	98	98	97	97	97	29
30	105	104	104	103	103	102	102	101	101	100	99	99	98	98	30
31	106	105	105	104	104	103	103	102	102	101	101	100	100	99	31
32	107	107	106	106	105	105	104	104	103	103	102	102	101	101	32
33	109	108	108	107	107	106	105	105	105	104	104	103	102	102	33
34	110	109	109	109	108	108	107	106	106	105	105	104	104	103	34
35	111	111	110	110	109	109	108	108	107	107	106	106	105	105	35
36	112	112	112	111	111	110	110	109	109	108	108	107	107	106	36
37	114	113	113	112	112	111	111	111	110	110	109	109	108	108	37
38	116	115	115	114	113	113	112	112	111	111	111	110	110	109	38
39	118	117	116	116	115	115	114	113	113	112	112	112	111	111	39
40	119	119	118	118	117	117	116	115	115	114	114	113	112	112	40
41	121	121	120	120	119	118	118	117	117	116	116	115	114	114	41
42	123	122	122	121	121	120	120	119	119	118	118	117	116	116	42
43	125	124	124	123	123	122	122	121	121	120	120	119	119	118	43
44	128	127	127	126	125	124	124	123	123	122	122	121	121	120	44
45			130	129	128	128	127	126	125	124	124	123	123	122	45
46							130	130	129	128	127	126	125	125	46
47												130	130	129	47
48															48
49															49
50															50
51															51
52															52
53															53
54															54
55						Award 131 for all scores in this area									55
	9:5	9:6	9:7	9:8	9:9	9:10	9:11	10:0	10:1	10:2	10:3	10:4	10:5	10:6	

Raw score	\multicolumn{13}{c	}{Age in years and completed months}	Raw score
	10:7	10:8	10:9	10:10	10:11	11:0	11:1	11:2	11:3	11:4	11:5	11:6	11:7	
1	\multicolumn{13}{c	}{Award 69 for all scores in this area}	1
2														2
3														3
4														4
5														5
6														6
7														7
8														8
9														9
10														10
11	71	70	70											11
12	73	73	72	71	71	70	70							12
13	75	75	74	74	73	72	72	71	71	70	70			13
14	77	76	76	75	75	74	74	73	73	72	72	71	71	14
15	78	78	77	77	76	76	76	75	75	74	73	73	72	15
16	79	79	78	78	78	77	77	76	76	76	75	75	74	16
17	81	80	80	79	79	79	78	78	77	77	77	76	76	17
18	82	82	81	81	80	80	79	79	79	78	78	77	77	18
19	83	83	82	82	81	81	81	80	80	79	79	79	78	19
20	84	84	83	83	83	82	82	81	81	81	80	80	79	20
21	86	85	85	84	84	83	83	83	82	82	81	81	80	21
22	87	87	86	86	85	85	84	84	83	83	82	82	82	22
23	89	88	88	87	87	86	86	85	84	84	84	83	83	23
24	90	89	89	88	88	88	87	87	86	85	85	84	84	24
25	91	91	90	90	89	89	88	88	87	87	86	86	85	25
26	93	92	92	91	90	90	89	89	89	88	88	87	87	26
27	94	93	93	93	92	91	91	90	90	89	89	88	88	27
28	95	95	94	94	93	93	92	92	91	90	90	89	89	28
29	96	96	95	95	94	94	94	93	93	92	91	91	90	29
30	97	97	96	96	96	95	95	94	94	93	93	92	92	30
31	99	98	98	97	97	96	96	95	95	95	94	94	93	31
32	100	100	99	98	98	97	97	97	96	96	95	95	94	32
33	101	101	101	100	99	99	98	98	97	97	96	96	96	33
34	103	102	102	101	101	100	100	99	99	98	98	97	97	34
35	104	104	103	103	102	102	101	101	100	100	99	98	98	35
36	106	105	105	104	104	103	103	102	102	101	101	100	100	36
37	107	107	106	106	105	105	104	104	103	103	102	102	101	37
38	109	108	108	107	107	106	106	105	105	104	104	103	103	38
39	110	110	109	109	108	108	107	107	106	106	105	105	104	39
40	112	111	111	110	110	109	109	108	108	107	107	106	106	40
41	113	113	112	112	111	111	110	110	110	109	109	108	108	41
42	115	115	114	114	113	112	112	112	111	111	110	110	109	42
43	117	117	116	116	115	115	114	113	113	112	112	111	111	43
44	120	119	118	118	117	117	116	116	115	114	114	113	113	44
45	122	121	121	120	120	119	119	118	117	117	116	116	115	45
46	124	124	123	123	122	122	121	121	120	119	119	118	118	46
47	128	127	126	125	125	124	124	123	123	122	122	121	121	47
48				130	129	128	128	127	126	125	124	124	123	48
49										130	129	129	128	49
50														50
51														51
52														52
53														53
54														54
55	\multicolumn{13}{c	}{Award 131 for all scores in this area}	55
	10:7	10:8	10:9	10:10	10:11	11:0	11:1	11:2	11:3	11:4	11:5	11:6	11:7	

GAPS 5 Spring: Age-standardised scores

GAPS 5 Summer: Age-standardised scores

Raw score	9:7	9:8	9:9	9:10	9:11	10:0	10:1	10:2	10:3	10:4	10:5	10:6	10:7	10:8	Raw score
1					Award 69 for all scores in this area										1
2															2
3															3
4															4
5															5
6															6
7	71	71	71	70	70	70	70								7
8	73	73	73	72	72	72	72	71	71	71	71	70	70	70	8
9	75	75	75	74	74	74	73	73	73	73	72	72	72	72	9
10	77	77	76	76	76	76	75	75	75	74	74	74	74	73	10
11	78	78	78	78	77	77	77	77	76	76	76	76	75	75	11
12	80	80	79	79	79	78	78	78	78	77	77	77	77	76	12
13	81	81	81	81	80	80	80	79	79	79	79	78	78	78	13
14	83	82	82	82	82	81	81	81	80	80	80	80	79	79	14
15	84	84	83	83	83	83	82	82	82	81	81	81	81	80	15
16	86	85	85	84	84	84	84	83	83	83	82	82	82	82	16
17	88	88	87	87	86	86	85	85	84	84	84	83	83	83	17
18	89	89	89	88	88	88	88	87	86	86	85	85	84	84	18
19	91	90	90	90	89	89	89	88	88	88	88	87	87	86	19
20	92	91	91	91	91	90	90	90	89	89	89	88	88	88	20
21	93	93	92	92	92	91	91	91	91	90	90	90	89	89	21
22	94	94	93	93	93	93	92	92	92	91	91	91	91	90	22
23	95	95	94	94	94	94	93	93	93	92	92	92	92	91	23
24	96	96	96	95	95	95	94	94	94	94	93	93	93	92	24
25	97	97	97	96	96	96	96	95	95	95	94	94	94	93	25
26	98	98	98	97	97	97	97	96	96	96	95	95	95	95	26
27	99	99	99	98	98	98	98	97	97	97	97	96	96	96	27
28	101	100	100	100	99	99	99	98	98	98	97	97	97	97	28
29	102	101	101	101	100	100	100	99	99	99	98	98	98	98	29
30	103	103	102	102	102	101	101	101	100	100	100	99	99	99	30
31	105	104	104	103	103	103	102	102	102	101	101	101	100	100	31
32	106	105	105	105	104	104	104	103	103	103	102	102	101	101	32
33	107	107	106	106	106	105	105	105	104	104	104	103	103	103	33
34	108	108	107	107	107	106	106	106	106	105	105	105	104	104	34
35	109	109	109	108	108	108	107	107	107	106	106	106	106	105	35
36	111	110	110	110	109	109	109	108	108	108	107	107	107	106	36
37	112	112	111	111	111	110	110	110	109	109	109	108	108	108	37
38	113	113	113	112	112	112	111	111	111	111	110	110	109	109	38
39	115	114	114	114	113	113	113	112	112	112	112	111	111	111	39
40	116	116	116	115	115	115	114	114	114	113	113	113	112	112	40
41	118	118	117	117	117	116	116	115	115	115	114	114	114	113	41
42	120	119	119	119	118	118	118	117	117	117	116	116	115	115	42
43	122	121	121	121	120	120	120	119	119	118	118	118	117	117	43
44	124	123	123	123	122	122	122	121	121	121	120	120	119	119	44
45	126	126	125	125	124	124	124	123	123	123	122	122	122	121	45
46	129	129	128	128	127	127	126	126	125	125	124	124	124	123	46
47						130	130	130	129	129	128	128	127	126	47
48														130	48
49															49
50															50
51															51
52															52
53															53
54															54
55					Award 131 for all scores in this area										55
	9:7	9:8	9:9	9:10	9:11	10:0	10:1	10:2	10:3	10:4	10:5	10:6	10:7	10:8	

Raw score	10:9	10:10	10:11	11:00	11:1	11:2	11:3	11:4	11:5	11:6	11:7	11:8	11:9	11:10	Raw score
1															1
2															2
3															3
4															4
5															5
6															6
7															7
8	70														8
9	71	71	71	71	70	70	70	70							9
10	73	73	72	72	72	72	71	71	71	71	70	70	70	70	10
11	75	74	74	74	74	73	73	73	72	72	72	72	71	71	11
12	76	76	76	75	75	75	75	74	74	74	73	73	73	73	12
13	78	77	77	77	77	76	76	76	76	75	75	75	74	74	13
14	79	79	78	78	78	78	77	77	77	77	76	76	76	76	14
15	80	80	80	79	79	79	78	78	78	78	77	77	77	77	15
16	81	81	81	81	80	80	80	79	79	79	79	78	78	78	16
17	83	82	82	82	81	81	81	81	80	80	80	80	79	79	17
18	84	83	83	83	83	82	82	82	82	81	81	81	80	80	18
19	85	85	84	84	84	83	83	83	83	82	82	82	82	81	19
20	88	87	87	86	85	85	84	84	84	83	83	83	83	82	20
21	89	88	88	88	88	87	87	86	85	85	84	84	84	83	21
22	90	90	89	89	89	88	88	88	88	87	86	86	85	85	22
23	91	91	90	90	90	90	89	89	89	88	88	88	87	87	23
24	92	92	92	91	91	91	90	90	90	90	89	89	89	88	24
25	93	93	93	92	92	92	91	91	91	91	90	90	90	89	25
26	94	94	94	93	93	93	93	92	92	92	91	91	91	91	26
27	95	95	95	94	94	94	94	93	93	93	92	92	92	92	27
28	96	96	96	96	95	95	95	94	94	94	93	93	93	93	28
29	97	97	97	97	96	96	96	95	95	95	95	94	94	94	29
30	98	98	98	98	97	97	97	97	96	96	96	95	95	95	30
31	100	99	99	99	98	98	98	97	97	97	97	96	96	96	31
32	101	100	100	100	99	99	99	98	98	98	98	97	97	97	32
33	102	102	101	101	101	100	100	100	99	99	99	98	98	98	33
34	104	103	103	102	102	102	101	101	101	100	100	100	99	99	34
35	105	105	104	104	104	103	103	102	102	102	101	101	101	100	35
36	106	106	106	105	105	105	104	104	104	103	103	102	102	102	36
37	107	107	107	106	106	106	106	105	105	105	104	104	104	103	37
38	109	108	108	108	107	107	107	107	106	106	106	105	105	105	38
39	110	110	110	109	109	108	108	108	107	107	107	107	106	106	39
40	112	111	111	111	110	110	110	109	109	109	108	108	108	107	40
41	113	113	112	112	112	112	111	111	111	110	110	110	109	109	41
42	115	114	114	114	113	113	113	112	112	112	112	111	111	111	42
43	117	116	116	115	115	115	115	114	114	114	113	113	113	112	43
44	119	118	118	118	117	117	116	116	116	115	115	115	114	114	44
45	121	121	120	120	119	119	119	118	118	118	117	117	116	116	45
46	123	123	122	122	122	121	121	121	120	120	120	119	119	118	46
47	126	125	125	124	124	124	123	123	123	122	122	122	121	121	47
48	130	129	129	128	128	127	127	126	126	125	125	124	124	124	48
49									130	130	129	129	128	128	49
50															50
51															51
52															52
53															53
54															54
55															55

Award 69 for all scores in this area (rows 1–7/8)

Award 131 for all scores in this area (rows 49/50–55)

GAPS 5 Summer: Age-standardised scores

GAPS 6 Autumn: Age-standardised scores

Raw score	10:1	10:2	10:3	10:4	10:5	10:6	10:7	10:8	10:9	10:10	10:11	11:0	11:1	Raw score
1					Award 69 for all scores in this area									1
2														2
3														3
4														4
5	70													5
6	73	72	72	71	71	70	70							6
7	76	75	75	74	73	73	72	72	72	71	71	70	70	7
8	78	78	77	77	76	76	75	75	74	73	73	72	72	8
9	81	80	80	79	78	78	77	77	76	76	75	75	74	9
10	83	82	82	81	81	80	80	79	79	78	77	77	76	10
11	85	84	84	83	83	82	82	81	81	80	80	79	78	11
12	86	86	85	85	84	84	83	83	82	82	81	81	80	12
13	88	87	87	86	86	85	85	85	84	84	83	83	82	13
14	89	89	88	88	87	87	86	86	85	85	85	84	84	14
15	90	90	89	89	89	88	88	87	87	86	86	85	85	15
16	91	91	91	90	90	89	89	88	88	88	87	87	86	16
17	93	92	92	91	91	90	90	90	89	89	88	88	88	17
18	94	94	93	93	92	92	91	91	90	90	89	89	89	18
19	96	95	95	94	94	93	92	92	91	91	91	90	90	19
20	97	97	96	96	95	95	94	93	93	92	92	91	91	20
21	98	98	97	97	96	96	95	95	94	94	93	92	92	21
22	100	99	99	98	98	97	97	96	96	95	95	94	93	22
23	101	100	100	99	99	98	98	97	97	96	96	95	95	23
24	103	102	101	101	100	100	99	99	98	98	97	96	96	24
25	104	103	103	102	102	101	100	100	99	99	98	98	97	25
26	105	105	104	104	103	102	102	101	101	100	99	99	98	26
27	106	106	106	105	104	104	103	103	102	101	101	100	100	27
28	107	107	107	106	106	105	105	104	103	103	102	102	101	28
29	109	108	108	107	107	106	106	105	105	104	104	103	102	29
30	110	109	109	108	108	107	107	106	106	106	105	104	104	30
31	111	111	110	110	109	108	108	107	107	107	106	106	105	31
32	112	112	111	111	110	110	109	109	108	108	107	107	106	32
33	114	113	113	112	112	111	111	110	109	109	108	108	107	33
34	115	115	114	113	113	112	112	111	111	110	110	109	109	34
35	117	116	116	115	114	114	113	113	112	112	111	111	110	35
36	118	117	117	116	116	115	115	114	114	113	112	112	111	36
37	119	119	118	118	117	117	116	116	115	114	114	113	113	37
38	122	121	120	119	119	118	118	117	117	116	115	115	114	38
39	124	123	123	122	121	120	119	119	118	117	117	116	116	39
40	127	126	125	124	123	122	122	121	120	119	118	118	117	40
41	129	129	128	127	126	125	124	123	122	122	121	120	119	41
42			130	130	129	128	127	126	125	124	124	123	122	42
43							130	129	128	127	126	126	125	43
44										130	130	129	128	44
45														45
46														46
47														47
48														48
49														49
50														50
51														51
52														52
53														53
54														54
55					Award 131 for all scores in this area									55
	10:1	10:2	10:3	10:4	10:5	10:6	10:7	10:8	10:9	10:10	10:11	11:0	11:1	

GAPS 6 Autumn: Age-standardised scores

Raw score	11:2	11:3	11:4	11:5	11:6	11:7	11:8	11:9	11:10	11:11	12:0	12:1	12:2	Raw score
					Age in years and completed months									
1					Award 69 for all scores in this area									1
2														2
3														3
4														4
5														5
6														6
7														7
8	72	71	71	70	70									8
9	74	73	73	72	72	71	71	70	70					9
10	76	75	75	74	74	73	73	72	72	71	71	70	70	10
11	78	77	77	76	76	75	75	74	74	73	73	72	72	11
12	80	79	79	78	78	77	77	76	76	75	74	74	73	12
13	82	81	81	80	79	79	78	78	77	77	76	76	75	13
14	83	83	82	82	81	81	80	80	79	78	78	77	77	14
15	85	84	84	83	83	82	82	81	81	80	80	79	78	15
16	86	85	85	85	84	84	83	83	82	82	81	81	80	16
17	87	87	86	86	85	85	84	84	83	83	82	82	82	17
18	88	88	87	87	87	86	86	85	85	84	84	83	83	18
19	89	89	89	88	88	87	87	86	86	85	85	85	84	19
20	90	90	90	89	89	88	88	88	87	87	86	86	85	20
21	91	91	91	90	90	89	89	89	88	88	87	87	86	21
22	93	92	92	91	91	90	90	90	89	89	88	88	88	22
23	94	94	93	92	92	91	91	91	90	90	89	89	88	23
24	95	95	94	94	93	93	92	92	91	91	90	90	89	24
25	97	96	96	95	95	94	93	93	92	92	91	91	90	25
26	98	97	97	96	96	95	95	94	94	93	92	92	91	26
27	99	99	98	98	97	96	96	95	95	94	94	93	93	27
28	100	100	99	99	98	98	97	97	96	96	95	95	94	28
29	102	101	101	100	99	99	98	98	97	97	96	96	95	29
30	103	103	102	101	101	100	100	99	99	98	98	97	96	30
31	105	104	104	103	102	102	101	100	100	99	99	98	98	31
32	106	105	105	104	104	103	102	102	101	101	100	99	99	32
33	107	106	106	106	105	105	104	103	103	102	101	101	100	33
34	108	107	107	107	106	106	105	105	104	104	103	102	102	34
35	109	109	108	108	107	107	106	106	106	105	105	104	103	35
36	111	110	110	109	109	108	108	107	107	106	106	105	105	36
37	112	112	111	111	110	109	109	108	108	107	107	107	106	37
38	114	113	113	112	111	111	110	110	109	109	108	108	107	38
39	115	115	114	114	113	112	112	111	111	110	110	109	109	39
40	117	116	116	115	115	114	113	113	112	112	111	111	110	40
41	118	118	117	117	116	116	115	115	114	113	113	112	112	41
42	121	120	119	119	118	118	117	116	116	115	115	114	114	42
43	124	123	122	121	120	119	119	118	118	117	117	116	116	43
44	127	126	125	124	123	122	122	121	120	119	118	118	117	44
45	130	129	129	128	127	126	125	124	123	122	121	120	119	45
46					130	129	129	128	127	126	125	124	123	46
47										130	129	128	127	47
48														48
49														49
50														50
51														51
52														52
53														53
54														54
55					Award 131 for all scores in this area									55
	11:2	11:3	11:4	11:5	11:6	11:7	11:8	11:9	11:10	11:11	12:0	12:1	12:2	

GAPS 6 Autumn: Age-standardised scores

GAPS 6 Spring: Age-standardised scores

Raw score	10:4	10:5	10:6	10:7	10:8	10:9	10:10	10:11	11:0	11:1	11:2	11:3	11:4	11:5	Raw score
1					Award 69 for all scores in this area										1
2															2
3															3
4															4
5															5
6															6
7	70														7
8	72	71	71	70	70										8
9	74	73	72	72	71	71	70	70							9
10	75	75	74	74	73	72	72	71	70	70					10
11	77	76	76	75	75	74	73	73	72	71	71	70	70		11
12	78	77	77	76	76	75	75	74	73	73	72	72	71	70	12
13	79	79	78	78	77	76	76	75	75	74	74	73	72	72	13
14	80	80	79	79	78	78	77	77	76	76	75	74	74	73	14
15	82	81	80	80	79	79	78	78	77	77	76	76	75	74	15
16	83	82	82	81	80	80	79	79	78	78	77	76	76	75	16
17	84	83	83	82	81	81	80	80	79	78	78	77	77	76	17
18	85	84	84	83	83	82	81	81	80	79	79	78	78	77	18
19	86	86	85	84	84	83	82	82	81	80	80	79	79	78	19
20	87	87	86	85	85	84	83	83	82	82	81	80	80	79	20
21	88	88	87	86	86	85	85	84	83	83	82	81	81	80	21
22	90	89	88	87	87	86	85	85	84	84	83	82	82	81	22
23	91	90	89	89	88	87	86	86	85	85	84	83	83	82	23
24	91	91	90	90	89	88	87	87	86	86	85	84	84	83	24
25	92	92	91	91	90	90	89	88	87	87	86	85	85	84	25
26	93	93	92	91	91	90	90	89	88	87	87	86	86	85	26
27	94	94	93	92	92	91	91	90	90	89	88	87	87	86	27
28	95	95	94	93	93	92	91	91	91	90	89	88	88	87	28
29	96	96	95	94	94	93	92	92	91	91	90	90	89	88	29
30	97	97	96	95	95	94	93	93	92	92	91	91	90	89	30
31	98	98	97	97	96	95	94	94	93	92	92	91	91	90	31
32	99	99	98	97	97	96	96	95	94	93	93	92	92	91	32
33	100	100	99	98	98	97	97	96	95	95	94	93	92	92	33
34	102	101	100	99	99	98	98	97	96	96	95	94	94	93	34
35	103	102	101	101	100	99	99	98	97	97	96	95	95	94	35
36	103	103	102	102	101	100	100	99	98	98	97	97	96	95	36
37	105	104	103	103	102	102	101	100	99	99	98	98	97	96	37
38	106	105	104	104	103	103	102	101	101	100	99	99	98	97	38
39	108	107	106	105	104	104	103	103	102	101	101	100	99	99	39
40	109	108	107	107	106	105	104	104	103	102	102	101	100	100	40
41	111	110	109	108	107	107	106	105	104	104	103	102	102	101	41
42	113	112	111	110	109	108	108	107	106	105	104	104	103	103	42
43	115	114	113	112	111	110	109	108	108	107	106	105	104	104	43
44	117	116	115	114	113	112	111	110	109	109	108	107	106	105	44
45	119	118	117	116	115	114	114	113	112	111	110	109	108	108	45
46	121	120	119	118	118	117	116	115	114	113	112	111	110	110	46
47	123	122	122	121	120	119	118	118	117	116	115	114	113	112	47
48	125	124	124	123	122	122	121	120	119	119	118	117	116	115	48
49	129	128	127	126	125	124	124	123	122	121	121	120	119	118	49
50					130	129	128	127	126	125	124	124	123	122	50
51									130	129	128	127	126	125	51
52															52
53															53
54															54
55					Award 131 for all scores in this area										55
	10:4	10:5	10:6	10:7	10:8	10:9	10:10	10:11	11:0	11:1	11:2	11:3	11:4	11:5	

Raw score	11:6	11:7	11:8	11:9	11:10	11:11	12:0	12:1	12:2	12:3	12:4	12:5	12:6	Raw score
1					Award 69 for all scores in this area									1
2														2
3														3
4														4
5														5
6														6
7														7
8														8
9														9
10														10
11														11
12	70													12
13	71	70	70											13
14	72	72	71	71	70									14
15	74	73	72	72	71	71	70							15
16	75	74	74	73	72	72	71	70	70					16
17	76	75	75	74	73	73	72	72	71	70	70			17
18	77	76	76	75	75	74	73	73	72	71	71	70	70	18
19	78	77	77	76	76	75	74	74	73	72	72	71	71	19
20	79	78	78	77	76	76	75	75	74	74	73	72	72	20
21	80	79	78	78	77	77	76	76	75	75	74	73	73	21
22	80	80	79	79	78	78	77	77	76	76	75	74	74	22
23	81	81	80	80	79	79	78	77	77	76	76	75	75	23
24	82	82	81	81	80	79	79	78	78	77	77	76	76	24
25	83	83	82	81	81	80	80	79	79	78	78	77	77	25
26	84	84	83	82	82	81	81	80	79	79	78	78	77	26
27	85	85	84	83	83	82	82	81	80	80	79	79	78	27
28	86	86	85	84	84	83	83	82	81	81	80	80	79	28
29	87	87	86	85	85	84	84	83	82	82	81	80	80	29
30	88	88	87	86	86	85	85	84	83	83	82	81	81	30
31	90	89	88	87	87	86	85	85	84	84	83	82	82	31
32	91	90	89	89	88	87	86	86	85	85	84	83	83	32
33	91	91	90	90	89	88	87	87	86	86	85	84	84	33
34	92	92	91	91	90	90	89	88	87	87	86	85	85	34
35	93	93	92	92	91	91	90	89	88	88	87	86	86	35
36	94	94	93	92	92	91	91	90	90	89	88	87	87	36
37	96	95	94	94	93	92	92	91	91	90	90	89	88	37
38	97	96	96	95	94	93	93	92	92	91	91	90	89	38
39	98	97	97	96	95	95	94	93	93	92	92	91	91	39
40	99	99	98	97	97	96	95	95	94	93	93	92	91	40
41	100	100	99	99	98	97	97	96	95	95	94	93	93	41
42	102	101	101	100	99	99	98	97	97	96	95	95	94	42
43	103	103	102	101	101	100	99	99	98	97	97	96	96	43
44	105	104	103	103	102	102	101	100	99	99	98	98	97	44
45	107	106	105	104	104	103	103	102	101	101	100	99	99	45
46	109	108	107	106	106	105	104	103	103	102	102	101	100	46
47	111	110	109	109	108	107	106	105	105	104	103	103	102	47
48	114	113	113	112	111	110	109	108	107	107	106	105	104	48
49	118	117	116	115	114	113	112	111	110	109	109	108	107	49
50	121	120	119	119	118	117	116	115	114	113	112	111	110	50
51	124	124	123	122	122	121	120	119	119	118	117	116	115	51
52		130	129	128	127	126	125	124	123	123	122	121	121	52
53											130	129	128	53
54														54
55					Award 131 for all scores in this area									55
	11:6	11:7	11:8	11:9	11:10	11:11	12:0	12:1	12:2	12:3	12:4	12:5	12:6	

GAPS 6 Spring: Age-standardised scores

GAPS 6 Summer: Age-standardised scores

Raw score	10:3	10:4	10:5	10:6	10:7	10:8	10:9	10:10	10:11	11:0	11:1	11:2	11:3	11:4	11:5	Raw score
1						Award 69 for all scores in this area										1
2																2
3																3
4																4
5	71	70														5
6	75	74	73	72	71	70										6
7	77	76	76	75	74	73	72	71	70	70						7
8	78	78	77	77	76	76	75	74	73	72	71	70	70			8
9	80	79	79	78	78	77	77	76	76	75	74	73	72	71	70	9
10	81	81	80	80	79	78	78	77	77	76	76	75	74	73	72	10
11	83	82	82	81	80	80	79	79	78	77	77	76	76	75	74	11
12	84	83	83	82	82	81	81	80	79	79	78	78	77	76	76	12
13	85	85	84	83	83	82	82	81	81	80	79	79	78	78	77	13
14	87	86	85	85	84	83	83	82	82	81	80	80	79	79	78	14
15	88	87	87	86	85	84	84	83	83	82	81	81	80	80	79	15
16	89	89	88	87	86	86	85	84	84	83	82	82	81	81	80	16
17	90	90	89	88	88	87	86	85	85	84	83	83	82	82	81	17
18	92	91	90	89	89	88	87	87	86	85	84	84	83	83	82	18
19	93	92	91	91	90	89	88	88	87	86	86	85	84	84	83	19
20	94	93	92	92	91	90	89	89	88	87	87	86	85	84	84	20
21	95	94	93	93	92	91	91	90	89	88	88	87	86	86	85	21
22	96	95	94	94	93	92	92	91	90	89	89	88	87	87	86	22
23	97	96	96	95	94	93	93	92	91	90	90	89	88	88	87	23
24	98	98	97	96	95	94	94	93	92	92	91	90	89	89	88	24
25	99	99	98	97	96	95	95	94	93	93	92	91	90	90	89	25
26	100	100	99	98	97	97	96	95	94	93	93	92	91	91	90	26
27	102	101	100	99	98	98	97	96	95	94	94	93	92	92	91	27
28	103	102	101	100	99	99	98	97	96	96	95	94	93	93	92	28
29	104	103	102	102	101	100	99	98	97	97	96	95	94	94	93	29
30	105	104	104	103	102	101	100	99	99	98	97	96	95	95	94	30
31	106	105	105	104	103	102	101	100	100	99	98	97	97	96	95	31
32	107	107	106	105	104	103	103	102	101	100	99	98	98	97	96	32
33	108	108	107	106	105	105	104	103	102	101	100	99	99	98	97	33
34	110	109	108	107	106	106	105	104	103	103	102	101	100	99	98	34
35	111	110	109	108	108	107	106	105	105	104	103	102	101	100	99	35
36	112	111	111	110	109	108	107	106	106	105	104	103	103	102	101	36
37	114	113	112	111	110	109	108	108	107	106	105	105	104	103	102	37
38	115	114	113	112	112	111	110	109	108	107	107	106	105	104	104	38
39	116	116	115	114	113	112	111	110	110	109	108	107	106	106	105	39
40	118	117	116	115	114	114	113	112	111	110	109	108	108	107	106	40
41	119	118	118	117	116	115	114	113	113	112	111	110	109	108	107	41
42	121	120	119	118	117	117	116	115	114	113	112	112	111	110	109	42
43	122	121	121	120	119	118	117	117	116	115	114	113	112	112	111	43
44	124	123	122	121	121	120	119	118	117	117	116	115	114	113	113	44
45	126	125	124	123	122	122	121	120	119	118	118	117	116	115	114	45
46	129	128	126	125	124	123	123	122	121	120	120	119	118	117	116	46
47			130	129	127	126	125	124	123	122	122	121	120	119	119	47
48						130	129	127	126	125	124	123	122	122	121	48
49									130	129	128	126	125	124	123	49
50												130	129	128		50
51																51
52																52
53																53
54																54
55						Award 131 for all scores in this area										55
	10:3	10:4	10:5	10:6	10:7	10:8	10:9	10:10	10:11	11:0	11:1	11:2	11:3	11:4	11:5	

Raw score	\multicolumn{14}{c	}{Age in years and completed months}	Raw score
	11:6	11:7	11:8	11:9	11:10	11:11	12:0	12:1	12:2	12:3	12:4	12:5	12:6	12:7	
1					\multicolumn{10}{l}{Award 69 for all scores in this area}	1
2															2
3															3
4															4
5															5
6															6
7															7
8															8
9															9
10	71	71	70												10
11	73	73	72	71	70										11
12	75	75	74	73	72	71	70								12
13	76	76	75	75	74	73	72	71	70						13
14	77	77	76	76	75	74	73	73	72	71	70				14
15	79	78	77	77	76	76	75	74	73	72	71	71	70		15
16	80	79	78	78	77	77	76	76	75	74	73	72	71	70	16
17	81	80	79	79	78	78	77	77	76	75	75	74	73	72	17
18	81	81	80	80	79	79	78	77	77	76	76	75	74	73	18
19	82	82	81	81	80	79	79	78	78	77	77	76	76	75	19
20	83	83	82	82	81	80	80	79	79	78	77	77	76	76	20
21	84	84	83	82	82	81	81	80	79	79	78	78	77	77	21
22	85	84	84	83	83	82	82	81	80	80	79	79	78	77	22
23	86	85	85	84	83	83	82	82	81	81	80	79	79	78	23
24	87	87	86	85	84	84	83	83	82	81	81	80	80	79	24
25	88	88	87	86	85	85	84	83	83	82	82	81	81	80	25
26	89	88	88	87	86	86	85	84	84	83	82	82	81	81	26
27	90	89	89	88	87	87	86	85	84	84	83	83	82	82	27
28	91	90	90	89	88	88	87	86	85	85	84	84	83	82	28
29	92	92	91	90	89	89	88	87	87	86	85	84	84	83	29
30	93	93	92	91	90	90	89	88	88	87	86	85	85	84	30
31	94	93	93	92	91	91	90	89	88	88	87	86	86	85	31
32	95	94	94	93	92	92	91	90	89	89	88	87	87	86	32
33	97	96	95	94	93	93	92	91	91	90	89	88	88	87	33
34	98	97	96	95	94	94	93	92	92	91	90	89	89	88	34
35	99	98	97	96	96	95	94	93	93	92	91	90	90	89	35
36	100	99	98	98	97	96	95	94	94	93	92	92	91	90	36
37	101	100	100	99	98	97	97	96	95	94	93	93	92	91	37
38	103	102	101	100	99	98	98	97	96	95	94	94	93	93	38
39	104	103	102	102	101	100	99	98	97	97	96	95	94	94	39
40	105	105	104	103	102	101	100	99	99	98	97	97	96	95	40
41	107	106	105	104	104	103	102	101	100	99	99	98	97	96	41
42	108	107	107	106	105	104	104	103	102	101	100	99	98	98	42
43	110	109	108	107	107	106	105	104	104	103	102	101	100	99	43
44	112	111	110	109	108	107	107	106	105	104	104	103	102	101	44
45	114	113	112	111	110	109	108	108	107	106	105	105	104	103	45
46	116	115	114	113	112	111	111	110	109	108	107	106	106	105	46
47	118	117	116	115	115	114	113	112	111	110	109	109	108	107	47
48	120	119	118	118	117	116	115	115	114	113	112	111	110	109	48
49	123	122	121	120	120	119	118	117	116	116	115	114	113	112	49
50	126	125	124	123	123	122	121	120	119	119	118	117	116	116	50
51			130	129	127	126	124	124	123	122	122	121	120	119	51
52									130	128	127	125	124	124	52
53															53
54															54
55					\multicolumn{10}{l}{Award 131 for all scores in this area}	55
	11:6	11:7	11:8	11:9	11:10	11:11	12:0	12:1	12:2	12:3	12:4	12:5	12:6	12:7	

GAPS 6 Summer: Age-standardised scores